Authentic Confidence

AUTHENTIC
CONFIDENCE

The SECRET to LOVING Your WORK
and LEADING an UNSTOPPABLE CAREER

BEN FAUSKE

NEW YORK

LONDON • NASHVILLE • MELBOURNE • VANCOUVER

AUTHENTIC CONFIDENCE

The Secret to Loving Your Work and Leading an
Unstoppable Career

Published in New York, New York, by Morgan James Publishing. Morgan James is a
trademark of Morgan James, LLC. www.MorganJamesPublishing.com

The content in this book does not act as a substitute for consulting with your local
physician or mental health professional. The author is not responsible for any loss
or damage allegedly arising from the material in this book. Individuals, groups
or organizations are listed for informational purposes. Listing does not imply an
endorsement. The author has made every effort to ensure accurate information and
does not assume any liability for errors or changes made after the publication.

ISBN 9781642797152 paperback
ISBN 9781642797169 eBook
Library of Congress Control Number: 2019945746

Cover and Interior Design by:
Chris Treccani
www.3dogcreative.net

Morgan James is a proud partner of Habitat for Humanity Peninsula
and Greater Williamsburg. Partners in building since 2006.

Get involved today! Visit
MorganJamesPublishing.com/giving-back

Dedicated to Kristy, Madison, Anna, Sydney, and Reese.
You inspire me every day. Thanks for your constant support.
I love you all.

Mom, Dad, and AJ, thanks for providing a great foundation
for my faith, my life, and my work.

Thanks to all my family near and far, for teaching
me the value of love and laughter.

CONTENTS

FOREWORD

t took me 20 years of success and failure on the world's largest stages to truly understand how confidence works. It's still very difficult for me to put into words. Ben Fauske does exactly that. His extensive studies and experience in this area are shared in this book and will provide a roadmap for your career. He addresses the confidence issues you didn't know you had.

To truly achieve Authentic Confidence, we must first accept the fact that we are all on a confidence journey. I've come to realize that any success I enjoyed in athletics and business was less about my physical or genetic attributes and more about my mental process. When Ben shared his Authentic Confidence process with me, it all made sense. He explained the dangers of over and under confidence. I have seen these dangers firsthand. Finding the appropriate amount of confidence is critical for success.

This book is about teaching you how to find the confidence that people feel, without having to be told. It is the confidence that draws people in, doesn't push them away. It is the confidence that gives you the power to take responsibility for your actions. It is the confidence necessary to accomplish your dreams.

I met Ben at the Center for Exceptional Leadership at St. Norbert College. At the time, I was the director of product strategies, leading a billion-dollar category for global dairy provider, Schreiber Foods. Schreiber had been working with

Ben for years adopting Authentic Confidence as a key process to develop talent. Hundreds of partners experienced the transformative coaching process provided in this book. The process works, and his mission to help leaders live and lead with confidence is obvious.

Confidence has been crucial to my progress as an athlete and leader. By the time I graduated high school, I had won nine national titles in three different styles of wrestling. At 19, I won a junior world title in Bucharest, Romania launching me onto the international scene. At 20, I became the youngest U.S. wrestler to ever make an Olympic team. Not only did I make the team; I won a bronze medal by beating a 5-time world champion from Russia.

After a second Olympics in Athens and several injuries, I was prematurely forced into retirement from wrestling at age 24. I spent the next year working through identity and confidence issues because I hadn't fully established who I was apart from wrestling. I needed to learn my strengths and weaknesses and determine what I would do next. At that point, I told myself that age 20 would not be the highlight of my career.

I decided my next adventure would be corporate leadership. I spent the next several years addressing my over and under confidence areas as my career progressed with Schreiber Foods. I have since acquired and built a multi-million-dollar portfolio of businesses. As these businesses evolve, I need to evolve as a leader. I do this by applying the Authentic Confidence process.

If you are interested in growing your influence or improving your culture, I recommend reading this book and applying the Authentic Confidence process.

Garrett Lowney
CEO and Olympic Medalist

PREFACE

You will likely work over 75,000 hours in your lifetime. How many will you enjoy? Confidence issues are often at the core of work challenges.

In this book, I will share proven strategies based on research, biology, and real-life stories that will transform your career. I have coached thousands of clients through the Authentic Confidence process and witnessed the leadership transformations. Whether you struggle with over or under confidence, this book will equip you with the tools to build an unstoppable career.

This book teaches you the mindset and game plan recording artists have been using for decades to find significant levels of success. It will provide you with a step-by-step process to build the career you deserve.

Why do so many rock stars keep working long after they could retire? The answer is simple. They have worked through their confidence issues and they love their work. We may not want to be rock stars, but there is no denying the value of moving from obscurity to influence.

The three steps to get the most out of this book are as follows:

1. Read the book and discover the core beliefs of people who love their work.

2. Increase your influence by learning how to communicate with Authentic Confidence.
3. Share the book with your team and start the confidence journey together.

You deserve to love your work, and loving your work is fundamental to loving life. Let's find the confidence to do it, together.

Ben Fauske
Creator and Coach
Authentic Confidence

INTRODUCTION

Why confidence? The topic is personal. My confidence issues used to be so bad that it led to recurring nightmares. During one nightmare, I was so terrified that I jumped out of bed and ran screaming into the other room. The problem is, before I made it to the other room, I ran face first into my dresser and it knocked me to the ground. Still half asleep, I felt blood running down my face. My wife woke me up and attempted to calm me down. I couldn't remember the details, but I knew these nightmares were not normal.

The previous day, I had gone for a walk. I had been struggling with my job for months and I was angry. I had already quit seven jobs in seven years, and I was about to quit number eight. I was fuming as I leaned into the arctic winds of Northeast Wisconsin. "How could I keep ending up here?" I vented to myself. I hated my work and couldn't handle my boss. I wondered if I were broken and couldn't be fixed. Maybe this was just my lot in life, to endure it.

I was so mad at myself for not being able to see my way out. Every job started out the exact same way. I was excited about the interview, I enjoyed hearing about the possibilities, and I loved learning about the potential impact I could make. I believed that I would make a difference and that hiring me would be one of the best decisions they ever made.

Then the same thing happened. I felt like I did not fit in the organization and I made the decision I couldn't work in that place one more day. The first few times I did this, I was justified. It was not my issue; it was "that place." Now it was obvious that I had issues.

This work depression impacted everything in my life. It affected my relationships with my family, who loved me, and it choked out friendships. It stopped my attempts to be healthy, as I had no ambition to be active. It even ruined my ability to sleep, due to recurring nightmares.

I had shortness of breath and a tight chest. I did not eat well, never exercised, and was irritated with everyone around me. The worst part is I felt that I deserved it. I was not good enough, I was not likable enough, and I wasn't OK.

I was so unsure of myself that I compensated by pretending to be strong even though I was scared. I was scared to lose my job, scared of being unemployed, and scared about being unable to provide for my family. I was scared of being found out as an incompetent fraud. I felt exposed and vulnerable, and this fear drove me to criticize others. If I could keep others on the defensive, then maybe I could keep the pressure off myself.

I made my rounds blaming coworkers, leaders, and dysfunctional teams. I had so many answers on what needed to be done—not from a place of helping but from a place of judging.

As I continued on my walk, the rage was overwhelming. So, under my breath, I started a rant, "Why was this happening to me? What had I done so wrong to deserve this?"

I remember feeling this sense of hopelessness after my tirade. The idea of enjoying work felt like a lie. In that moment, I realized it came down to a choice for me: "Am I going to give up or dig in?" It was a question that kept me up at night. I was drowning and couldn't find a way out. I realized I had a choice. Would I give up on my career dreams and just numb out, or would I dig in and find a new path?

I somehow knew this decision would shape the rest of my career. One path would lead to career boredom and one to finding answers. The only problem was that I had no idea how to find the answers.

A trusted family friend told me that finding the path for his career was not easy but worth the effort. He was successful and I could tell he had something I desperately wanted. When I asked him the secret, he did not have any direct solutions.

He recommended that I start reading autobiographies from individuals who loved their work. He explained that he found tremendous value in learning from other leaders. He suggested I find leaders that I admired and learn what they did to find success and perhaps I would find what I was missing.

So, I began. I started reading about business leaders, spiritual leaders, historical leaders, and sports legends. At first, it was overwhelming as I seemed to be finding contradictory advice. So much of what I learned depended on that leader's situation. I would read about Mother Teresa in the morning and Jack Welch at night, and I was confused. Many leaders gave opposite advice.

Then I found a group that connected to my situation: recording artists. No matter how famous a musician's parents or family, all of them had to make it on their own. This is what I wanted, and I decided to focus my efforts on recording artists. After reading hundreds of books and watching thousands of interviews, I discovered a pattern.

Every musician I admired followed this pattern to work through their confidence issues and find success. This pattern changed the trajectory of my career. I realized that my confidence issues had been holding me back, and I now had a roadmap to address those challenges.

I went from hating my work to learning to love it. I had hope in my career for the first time. I started looking forward to going in to work, and I felt energized. What I learned changed my ability to enjoy my family, friends, and gave me hope for the future. I finally had a blueprint that worked. I couldn't believe how different I felt. I started experiencing a success I never thought possible. That is why I wrote this book. I wanted to share this pattern with you.

Before I explain the process, I want to clarify who I hope will read this book.

During my writing, I pictured the person who might need help with the following:

Are you feeling anxious or stressed at work?

Do you feel like a fake or imposter at work?

Are you struggling to get along with your boss or coworkers?

Do you feel you lack the education or experience needed for future success?

Do you feel misunderstood or undervalued?

Do you struggle with public speaking?

Do you want to increase your influence?

Do you feel like you are falling behind where you should be?

Do you struggle with a lack of results by others?

Would you like to learn how to coach confidence in others?

If you answered yes to any of these questions, then this book is for you.

I will share the research and scientific evidence that explains the fact that we all have confidence issues and provides proven ways to work through those challenges. You also will hear real-world stories from the individuals and organizations I have coached through this process. I believe we are all on a confidence journey.

This book was written for people who want to find confidence for themselves or coach confidence in others. If you are not interested in finding or sharing confidence with others, please give this book as a gift to someone who needs it.

If you are like me and have some issues, please join me on the journey toward Authentic Confidence. This process will teach you how to love your work and create the unstoppable career you deserve.

The Authentic Confidence Process has three phases:

Phase I is the Core Beliefs phase. Here, I will share the core beliefs you need in order to love your work. I will also explain Authentic Confidence and why it is important in your career.

Phase II is called Self-Assessment. In this phase, you learn about the Confidence Profiles and complete the Authentic Confidence Quotient. In this confidential self-

assessment, you will grow in self-awareness and learn your current level of confidence, your limiting beliefs, and future career goals.

Phase III is Career Building. Here, you will identify one core confidence issue and create a game plan to resolve it. This is the secret pattern followed by recording artists. Here, you will have a game plan for the rest of your career.

My hope is that you find meaningful work and are valued for what you deliver. It will be challenging, but it will be worth it. This pattern works for new leaders, coaches, clergy, physicians, nurses, bankers, lawyers, construction supervisors, sales professionals, plant employees, engineers, executives, athletes, and any position that requires strong leadership.

Phase I: Core Beliefs

Why Some Love and Others Hate Work

AUTHENTIC CONFIDENCE OVERVIEW:

- The number one currency in every organization is **customer confidence.**

- The top driver for customer confidence is **engaged talent.**

- Talent is engaged or disengaged primarily through their **direct supervisor.**

- **Supervisors** who communicate with Authentic Confidence build **unstoppable careers and teams.**

- **Authentic Confidence** is defined as: **Pride in Work + Humility in Relationships.**

- **Coaching Authentic Confidence is the highest form of influence.**

AUTHENTIC CONFIDENCE MODEL:

Investing in yourself is always the right thing to do and it starts with
Authentic Confidence.

CHAPTER 1

The Loss of Customer Confidence

How many employees does it take to ruin an organization's reputation?

Several years ago, my wife Kristy and I decided to take our two oldest girls on a trip to the Magic Kingdom in Disney World. My parents took me when I was young, and the experience was amazing. However, that was almost 30 years ago, and I worried that Disney might seem a bit run down or feel outdated.

I could not have been more wrong. It was amazing to watch Disney's passionate staff interact with my daughters. They were down at eye level with them, presenting "first time visitor" badges and thanking them for coming to visit. My girls were treated like princesses and I opened my wallet at every turn, enjoying the experience as much as they were. It is crazy to think of all the promises Disney makes about creating a magical environment. They were living up to the billing.

Now, as an organizational development consultant, I must admit, part of me was looking for a flaw in the system. Where do they struggle as an organization? What is it that they should be working on? Come on, everyone needs help somewhere, right? Even the almighty Disney cannot be perfect...

Well, I found nothing. From what I could see, there wasn't a single thing from a leadership or culture standpoint that needed work—that was until our shuttle drive home on the third night.

It was late. The shuttle was packed, and everyone was tired. There were two doors on the shuttle, one in the front and one in the back. Because there were so many customers looking to ride, people entered the shuttle at both sets of doors, even though it was clearly marked to enter only at the front. The driver was not happy that people were entering through the back doors. He continually reminded people to enter the shuttle through the front only.

The shuttle eventually had standing room only and Kristy and I were in the back with our daughters sleeping on our shoulders. At the stop before ours, we stepped off through the back door and then walked back on through the back doors.

That was it for the driver; he lost it and yelled, "That is an exit only! You CANNOT enter through the back doors! YOU MUST use the FRONT DOORS!" Suddenly, there was a mutiny on board, because everyone knew we were just trying to help other passengers get off the shuttle. People started yelling back at the driver. "They were just TRYING to help, but I guess you don't care about that! Yeah, welcome to Disney! Nice attitude, Buddy!" Kristy and I attempted to settle things down.

We just wanted to get back to our room and crash. It had been a long day.

Secretly, however, I was thinking, *Ha, they are not perfect. They have flaws just like everyone else.* I took some comfort in knowing not even Disney had it all together all the time. As Kristy and I finally exited the shuttle at our stop, the driver also got out of the shuttle and walked toward us. Now, I had been very nice up to this point, but if he thought he was going to yell at us some more, well then, he was going to see a different side of me. I may be small, but I am wiry, and if he wanted a battle, he was going to get one. I wondered if the only memory our girls would have is their dad getting beaten up by a Disney shuttle driver.

I also remember thinking that this one person could ruin our experience.

When he walked up to us, he said, "I just want to apologize for the way I handled that situation earlier. My behavior was unacceptable and it's not what we do here at Disney."

I was speechless at first—completely thrown off. That was not what I was expecting. I replied, "Don't worry about it; it's not a big deal."

He responded, "No, it is a big deal. Is there anything I can do to make it up to you?"

I said, "No, we're good. Thank you for coming to talk to us."

We walked away in shock. When we think back to that trip, there were many great memories and experiences, but we will never forget that shuttle driver. The driver was able to own his behavior and show a genuine humility that left a lasting impression. His openness to the feedback turned a negative into a positive, and this is often the case with an honest apology.

He could have ruined the Disney reputation for us. Instead, he enhanced their reputation. What would our world look like if everyone demonstrated this type of leadership? Imagine if every organization were filled with that level of commitment.

This driver demonstrated an amazing level of self-awareness. He was in the middle of an emotional and confrontational state, yet he was able to view his role objectively, and realize things were not going well and redirect the conversation. At that moment, my confidence in Disney skyrocketed. I already trusted them, and this event solidified that trust. Why? We all have bad days, and to see someone demonstrate that level of commitment proved to me that their culture is real.

The other reason this story sticks with me is because of this rare moment. Most organizations are struggling to create an engaging culture.

Organizational culture is defined as the work environment created by leaders. The culture is discovered by understanding the written and unwritten rules that govern behavior. Culture has an enormous impact on customer confidence.

Why do organizations exist? This was a question debated by one of my clients in the financial sector. We were in a board meeting and the discussion was heated. Some board members were passionately explaining the organization exists to make money. Others stated the purpose was to serve customers. There was an elder statesman of the board who had been quiet the entire conversation. Finally, he started to speak, and the room became very quiet. He ran the largest organization in the area and had seen unprecedented success in his tenure. He shared a story. "When I was growing up, we would sit around the dinner table and discuss the family business. My parents shared this belief: If we take care of our customers, they will take care of us. We will be seeing our friends and neighbors in the grocery store, at football games, and other community events. We must be able to look them square in the eyes and know we treated them fairly. If our goal is simply to make money, they will feel that. If they know our goal is to provide them great products at a fair price, they will feel that as well. If our customers feel we gave them a great value, then we will all win in the end." The discussion was over. Everyone understood the wisdom and agreed.

In any organization, customer confidence is the most important currency. Why is customer confidence so valuable? Disney promises a magical experience, and they deliver. We are willing to pay for promises delivered.

The relationship we have with our customers is based on authenticity and trust. If customers lose confidence, organizations go out of business. Every customer has options for the products and services they buy. If employees are disengaged, customers often have a negative experience. They will eventually lose confidence and take their business with them.

One major retailer recently felt the sting of customers losing confidence. Shopko Corporation was founded in 1962 and had 18,000 employees in 2018 before Chapter 11 bankruptcy on January 16, 2019.

I walked into one of the locations after declaring bankruptcy and I chatted with an employee. She was sitting on the patio furniture looking down at her phone. It was obvious that she was shocked and heartbroken. When I asked her what happened, she said, "People stopped caring." She went on to share, "When I started at Shopko many years earlier, everyone had a pride in their work. We were all busy making this a great place to work.

We knew our customers were loyal and wouldn't shop anywhere else because they loved the Shopko experience. The staff was friendly, and we cared about each other. Somewhere along the way, we lost that. I'm not surprised, just sad, and I'm not sure what I'm going to do next."

How does customer confidence work? I will use a medical analogy to explain how we make decisions as a customer. (Disclaimer: This example is not meant to be medically accurate, but to illustrate confidence issues.)

In this scenario, you need heart surgery and you are going to choose one of three surgeons. They fit into the following categories: Over Confidence (OC), Under Confidence (UC), or Authentic Confidence (AC). You will meet with each one individually and then make your decision.

Type 1: Dr. OC

The over confident surgeon walks in with an arrogant swagger and says, "This is your lucky day. I don't even know how you got on my schedule, as I have a waiting list of two years. You're welcome in advance, because I guarantee you; I am the best at what I do. I don't have time for your questions right now; please talk with my nurse. See you for surgery prep next week."

Type 2: Dr. UC

The under confident surgeon shuffles into the room, head down, and says, "Well, I know you're probably worried, and I'm also a bit freaked out. I just graduated last night, online, and I just can't believe how many valves the heart has—so crazy. I've never done this procedure before, but I watched a bunch of YouTube videos last night. I'm willing to give it a try. What do you think? If you don't want to proceed, I understand. So, will I see you next week for surgery?"

Type 3: Dr. AC

The surgeon with Authentic Confidence walks in, looks you straight in the eye, and gives you a firm handshake. After answering your questions, Dr. AC might share some final thoughts, "I've successfully completed this procedure thousands of times. I understand you may have more questions before the surgery, and we'll be here to answer them. We have a great team and we're prepared. You're in good hands, and I look forward to chatting with you again at surgery prep next week."

I know this is an absurd example, but who would you choose?

Over Confidence

Individuals who are over confident may be really good at what they do, but they are tough to be around. If customers have to make a choice they would choose over confidence before under confidence, but they are not happy about it. As soon as they can find a better option, they will take it. Over confident behaviors appear insensitive, arrogant, and bossy. Their behaviors are toxic in a team setting.

For example, one of the clients I worked for had not admitted to a mistake in over 30 years. The impact on his team was that no one would give him feedback. They learned early on that any attempt to help this guy would be met with a cold glare, at best. His behavior created multiple issues including a stalemate on the team, high turnover, and low morale. He was sending the message that he was too good for feedback, and his solution was the only solution. After working with him for a few months, he finally embraced his over confidence bias and decided he wanted to lead differently.

He sat down with his team, and for the first time said, "I need help with feedback. I don't receive it enough, and I would like to become better at asking for it and then acting on it." He then asked his team to help him process feedback in the future. I thought his coworkers' jaws were going to hit the table. They had never heard anything like this from him before and for the first time in decades, they had hope—hope that their team engagement would improve, hope that their boss had changed for good, and hope that they would be able to build the type of relationship they had always wanted with him.

Under Confidence

Individuals who are under confident demonstrate behaviors that are often fear based and indecisive. Customers will do whatever they can to avoid this option. Under confident behaviors are unsettling. Individuals with under confidence often worry about the opinion of others and feel that they are not good enough. These behaviors are also disruptive in a team setting.

For example, one of my clients would react at her worst whenever her competence was challenged. She would turn red in the face and move into attack mode. After each encounter, she would be filled with regret and shame.

This pattern repeated. She suffered, and so did her career. Once she understood the impact of her under confidence and what triggered those negative behaviors, she was able to map out ways to respond differently. She was not perfect at it. Change takes practice, but once she realized that she could take a breath and control her response, both the quality of her relationships and her influence drastically improved.

Over confidence and under confidence are career-crippling behaviors. Conversely, Authentic Confidence is the fast track to success. Leaders with Authentic Confidence exhibit two critical traits: pride and humility. These traits may seem to oppose each other, but in the right balance, they are a powerful combination.

Authentic Confidence

Customers are attracted to the individual with Authentic Confidence. They will be loyal and invested in this interaction. They believe it is the best solution and will spread the message in convincing fashion. They deliver exceptional service and create great relationships.

Most decisions are not life and death like the heart surgeon example; however, the choices remain. Every customer will continually look for the option of Authentic Confidence until they find it.

Maybe you do not believe you are as important as a heart surgeon, or that you have the ability to inspire a city, but be careful not to diminish your role. You are designed to make an impact. No one else can deliver your unique contribution. If you deliver it with Authentic Confidence, you will be building your career on a solid foundation.

Early in my career, I experienced leaders with significant confidence issues. I witnessed customers leaving due to over and under confident behaviors. Once this started happening, employees were the next to leave.

Communicating the appropriate amount of confidence is contagious, and getting it wrong is costly. Unfortunately, I witnessed few leaders getting it right. Musicians were a group I found most interesting in this regard. They had to work through their confidence issues and had a unique relationship with their fans. They clearly understood the connection between their work and customer confidence.

Whey they take the stage, they understand their connection to the fans. British rocker Johnny Marr believes that every ticket sold is an individual contract with that fan. He has an obligation to give his best every show. Customers feel that connection and are loyal and willing to pay the ticket price, based on that agreement.

Professional golfer, Jack Nicklaus once said, "Confidence is the most important single factor in this game, and no matter how great your natural talent, there is only one way to obtain and sustain it: work."

Jack played the game of golf, and he also built a successful golf course construction business. He understood the power of his role, and he took his work seriously. He influenced millions of people throughout his professional career. He knew the fans were paying to see a great show, and he ensured he was prepared to perform at every event. This commitment to be his authentic self and delivering an exceptional experience for the fans was essential to his success.

CHAPTER 2

We are NOT Engaged...

Disengagement is the root cause of work hate. I recently heard a retiree say, "I have 1,334 days, 3 hours and 17 minutes until retirement." He was talking about work as if it were a prison sentence. Unfortunately, this is all too common. Passing the time until retirement is no way to live. If everyone wins when employees are engaged, why aren't they? Employee engagement is defined as how passionate employees feel about their work and how committed they are to the organization. If organizations are filled with engaged employees, they are filled with loyal and confident customers. Unfortunately, most employees are not engaged. I have been working with leaders and teams in both big and small corporations for years, and they provide great examples of Authentic Confidence. When I start working with an organization on engagement, I always ask two questions:

What characteristics describe a great team?
What characteristics describe a terrible team?

When I ask what makes great teams, I often hear answers like "high expectations," "competence," and "strong leadership." In other words, leaders have to be strong but not too strong. Confidence, done correctly, creates an environment where everyone thrives.

Unfortunately, most organizations do not create cultures to help people get it right.

Negative behaviors in teams are often related to confidence issues. Ego, hidden agendas, and selfish behaviors always generate the strongest reactions. Over confident behaviors by coworkers are often listed as the root cause of terrible teams. Working on a terrible team is the most common reason people hate work. Confidence done wrong is a problem and creates an unhealthy environment.

The Gallup Company has been conducting research for over 75 years and has found that more than 70% of the American workforce is disengaged. This is a shocking statistic, but what is even more shocking is that new employees are almost always engaged.

If you talk to someone starting a new job, they typically cannot wait for the new opportunity. Yet, soon, two out of three will end up disengaged. This is an epidemic with disastrous consequences.

Early in my career, I fit this description. My negative work experiences impacted my family, my friends, and my health. I was miserable, and when I looked around, it was obvious I was not alone. I knew plenty of people who disliked their work and were functioning in survival mode. That is not what anyone wants. I do not believe people start off choosing to be disengaged; I believe their environment is filled with unresolved confidence issues.

I don't know Barry Bonds, and he might behave differently now, but this story demonstrates how confidence issues impact the culture of a team. I have no judgment of Barry; I just want to use the San Francisco Giants baseball team as an example.

August 7, 2007, should have been one of the greatest moments in baseball history. Barry Bonds broke Hank Aaron's home run record of 755, and it should have been an event that would inspire future generations of baseball players. But many fans were not inspired. He broke the record, but it appeared that even his teammates were not celebrating. They were not engaged. Why?

Barry Bonds was a great baseball player, yet most fans were turned off by his selfish attitude. He did not just alienate fans; he also alienated most of his team. His own teammate, Jeff Kent, told *Sports Illustrated* in 2002, "On the field, we're fine, but, off the field, I don't care about Barry and Barry doesn't care about me or anybody." Sadly, this type of "I am better than you" attitude is one of the most repelling behaviors in any field. It is why many people hate their work. They spend every day in an environment filled with gossip when certain people are only looking out for themselves. Nobody likes a showoff, yet it is a common behavior in business, sports, and politics.

There are many reasons why confidence issues are left unchecked. The person with the confidence issues might be a great performer, as in the case of Barry Bonds. Leaders are afraid to address the issue, because this star player may leave. The perceived fear of the organization being shut down or never recovering from such a loss is perceived to be real. Members of the team may attempt to deal with the issues, but they are quickly shut down by the person with the confidence issues.

If they keep failing in their attempts to help that person change their behaviors, they eventually give up. You hear things like, "That's just Barry." It is not a safe environment to discuss confidence issues, so everyone ignores the problem, and everyone suffers for it. This, in turn, increases the confidence issues of everyone else on the team.

When one person demonstrates over confidence, others will have to demonstrate under confident behaviors to survive. In other words, if Barry says, "Do this or I'll leave," everyone around him has to bow down to his wishes."

Instead of a balance of opinions, there is one dominant and many submissive team members. Instead of dealing with the problem behaviors directly, the team decides to talk about those behaviors behind the dominant person's back. Healthy individuals do not want to do this, but it often feels like their only safe option. This breaks down trust and creates dysfunctional teams. Where gossip thrives, so does disengagement.

Comparison Kills Confidence

Our current culture is hyper-focused on comparison. Social media creates temporary confidence. If people make a post and it garners the right amount of "likes," then they feel good about themselves. Their self-esteem is boosted, and all is right with the world. If the post does not receive enough attention, they feel down and enter depressive thinking. They may wonder, *what is wrong with my post?*, *why don't people like me?* or *will I ever measure up?* These are harmful questions, as they are dependent on the actions of others. We live in a culture where the constant comparison of followers, likes, and shares dictates our perceived relevance.

This thinking leads to jealousy and fragility. People are one post away from losing their social status. Likes have been proven to release endorphins in the brain, which creates a response similar to drug addiction. People are addicted to the likes. If they are having a bad day, they will make a post and create a false sense of confidence. These virtual "likes" transfer to some form of affirmation, and they will think, "I am a good and likable person." This false sense of self is addictive and not sustainable. This translates into work, as every project must be endorsed by others.

In the past, no news was good news. If you were hired and did not hear anything, you assumed, you were doing well. Now, no news is bad news. If new employees are not receiving continual feedback, they fear they are not doing well. When instant feedback is the norm, it is difficult for managers to reassure employees they are doing well. When confidence is based on external factors, employees will always feel unsettled. External confidence is temporary and dangerous. When employees live in the comparison game, there will always be someone who is working harder and achieving more desirable results.

Early in my career, I was worried about how I measured up to others. I realized living in comparison was a great way to guarantee disappointment. There is a strategy to move out of disengagement, and it is explained in The Engagement Cycle.

THE ENGAGEMENT CYCLE

The Engagement Cycle moves from Influence to Blame to Ownership. This is a naturally occurring cycle that we will all move through in our career. Most employees start a new job in the influence phase. They attempt to make a positive impact and improve things. When their suggestions are not handled well, they move to self-blame. They may think to themselves, *I must not have good ideas, No one cares about my opinion,* or *What I say doesn't matter.*

Next, they move on to blaming others. They may say to themselves, "They don't get it," or "There is something wrong with the organization, with the leaders, with my teammates." Eventually, they give up. This disengagement then translates to customers. When employees blame the organization for the inability to do their work, customers sense that. This incongruence turns loyal customers into skeptics.

Why is blame so toxic? When employees blame the organization, customers feel stuck in the middle. They have to choose their alliance between the person and the organization. The ideal customer experience is when the employee loves working for that organization. The customer can then embrace the person and the brand.

Blame typically originates from a perceived lack of fairness. Individuals think they are right and others are wrong. There is often a hyper-focus on what others are doing. Let's slow the blame process down and look at why it exists.

I started seeing the results of blame when I was a counselor, responsible for some marital counseling. When a couple was struggling, I would hear blame language. When I would separate the two and speak with them individually, I noticed an interesting response. I would ask the husband who was to blame in the relationship, and he would say his wife. He would explain all the things he had done for her and she had done nothing in return. I would then ask what percent his wife was to blame. He would often say 100%. Then I would ask him to step out of the office, and I would talk to his wife. The same scenario would unfold. So, both parties believed it was 100% the other person's fault. The other person was to blame, and as soon as that person got their act together, things would be fine.

The interesting question that I would pose to them is "What is your 1%?" This question was rarely well received. They would say things like, "What do you mean, what is my 1%?" They would remind me that I did not know how infuriating it was to be married to this person. After all of their excuses and complaining they would finally share the 1%. What followed was always fascinating. The husband would start with something like, "Well I work too much and don't spend enough time with her." When he would admit his 1%, his body language would change. His shoulders would slump, and he would become quiet. It was as if he were done fighting with me about his wife and realized that he also contributed to the relationship not working. It was a move to the ownership phase of The Engagement Cycle. I believe much of the blame of others comes after we blame ourselves. He knew he was not being the husband she deserved. He knew that he was being selfish at times and putting his own needs before hers in an unhealthy way. Yet why would he choose to spend so much of his life blaming himself.

In other words, if he came home late from work and was feeling a healthy amount of guilt on the way home, he was entering into self-blame. He might be thinking, "I'm always late, I don't spend the time with her that I should. Why am I working so hard anyway; isn't it for her?" Then when he gets home and starts to apologize and is in a vulnerable position, his wife starts blaming him. "No surprise, you're late again, dinner is cold again and the family ate dinner without you again!"

It is hard in those moments to say, "You're right; I'm sorry." So, instead, the husband reorganizes his thoughts and responds with "Well, I was working for us; you're so ungrateful for the sacrifices I make." All of this happens in a split second. There is no discussion as to how either side is really feeling, and both are entrenched in blame.

If they were honest, they would say, "I wish we could spend more time together and stick to our commitments to each other. I feel excluded and alone when you don't make our relationship a priority." Instead, they retreat to their corners, and when provoked, come out swinging.

If he were able to remain in the vulnerable position and take ownership for his actions, they may be able to work it through, but retreating and blaming is the habitual option they have chosen to survive. Then, eventually, when their relationship is based on blame, there is little room left for forgiveness or second chances.

When he would own his 1%, there would often be moments of deep reflection. The first step is helping him understand that although his behavior was not the best, self-blame is not the answer. No relationship is based on achieving perfection; it is about progress.

Once he found a way to apologize and own his 1%, his wife would often do the same, and then we had something to talk about.

The same is true for leadership. We must first understand our self-blame, and how we blame others, before we can move back into ownership.

When an individual works hard to move them back to ownership, often, others will follow. Comments such as, "Focus on what you can control," and "Keep a positive attitude about your work," are all attempts to reengage the person. The hope is that the person might start enjoying the work and seeing progress. Inevitably, they will have some ideas to improve aspects of the organization. They might go back to influence, thinking they can make a difference again. They might be willing to give it one more shot. They share this idea, but this time, they were more strategic about it. They spent more time thinking it through and are more convinced it is a good idea.

Then again, if it does not go well, they will realize the culture does not support them. Now the person feels angry, and they will go back to blame. They learn that engagement is too painful. It is not worth it for them to put their heart and soul into their work. So they check out—maybe for good.

The negative experiences snowball, and they believe no matter what they do, nothing will ever change. Convincing this person to reengage now is no small task. They have a history of emotional experiences that tell them to keep their distance. They may not quit, but they are certainly wounded.

They may be nice and cordial in meetings, but as soon as the meeting is done, they have a follow-up meeting where the real issues are discussed and gossiped about. This is an entrenched culture of disengagement.

Most organizations struggle with how they should engage these employees. They want employees to lead well, but the employee engagement strategies do not work.

The problem is simple. Many organizations spend time and money surveying employees without seeing results. Employee engagement consultants are gifted at taking the temperature, but do not know how to change the climate. Handling confidence issues is tough, and that is why consultants avoid this crucial step.

Employees are exhausted with continually answering the same questions and seeing no change. The reason why most consultants focus their energy on the survey, is that building leaders is hard work, but that is also where the change happens. When leaders understand their confidence issues and can discuss them in a safe way, everyone wins. Confidence issues are tricky, so creating a safe environment in which to discuss them is crucial.

Why do musicians still record new music and tour long after they have achieved financial security? They do not need to work, yet they still perform. The research is overwhelming. The reason artists still go through all of the difficulty of recording and traveling is because they love the work. They are in the influence stage of their careers and they enjoy the moments they co-create with their audiences. A dynamic relationship exists between the fans and the artists. They understand delivering great music is the best way to say thank you to their fans. They do not stop because they do not want to stop.

Imagine if that were true of everyone in your organization. Working because they loved it and enjoyed the impact their work had on others.

CHAPTER 3

Culture is the Problem

History is filled with the horrors of comparison. "We are better than you," is a dangerous statement. World wars and genocide have been started based on that statement. In order to combat the dangers of tyrannical leaders, countries have decided to focus on the power of culture. An organization's culture is the most powerful force in shaping individual behavior. The culture is the unwritten rules of an organization that determines appropriate behavior. One cultural philosophy that was created to deal with over confident tendencies is called the Law of Jante. The Law of Jante is from Danish and Norwegian author Aksel Sandemose and impacts organizations and societies around the world today. He wrote a book in the 1930s called *A Fugitive Crosses His Tracks* and covered this Nordic code of conduct. He created the 10 rules, but the concepts had been in place in Scandinavian culture for centuries.

The Law of Jante:

1. You're not to think you are anything special.
2. You're not to think you are as good as we are.
3. You're not to think you are smarter than we are.
4. You're not to imagine yourself better than we are.
5. You're not to think you know more than we do.
6. You're not to think you are more important than we are.
7. You're not to think you are good at anything.
8. You're not to laugh at us.
9. You're not to think anyone cares about you.
10. You're not to think you can teach us anything.

There is also an 11th rule that is the penalty for not following one of these 10 rules.

11. Perhaps you don't think we know a few things about you?

Sandemose wrote these rules to explain what was happening. He did not intend these rules to guide behavior, but rather to describe it.

In this culture, everyone is concerned about the unchecked ego. These 11 laws attempt to keep people humble. Some believe these 11 rules have attributed to happiness and teaching people to be content with what they have. Others have said it has done just the opposite and has led to mental health problems. It enforces the belief that you have nothing special to share with the world. This is depressive thinking and, if left unattended, could lead to self-harm.

In 2018, Swedish actor Alexander Skarsgard explained the Laws of Jante, also known as Janteloven. He had recently won an Emmy and a Golden Globe. When asked how he would celebrate his achievements, he said that was an uncomfortable topic for him. He was embarrassed with the compliments he received about his accomplishments. He was proud of his work yet had to work very hard to make sure he was not bragging to anyone about it. If he would, he would be put back in place by his community. In his country, you do not boast about such things. He even joked he did not know where to place his Emmy and Golden Globe trophies, as he could never display them in his house because that would make him appear arrogant. In Sweden, if you say you are a good tennis player, you better be one of the best in the world, or you are lying. They believe the communal benefits of remaining humble far outweigh the individual detriments of suppressing success. In other words, they would rather have a humble community than displays of individual happiness.

This Nordic tradition is in my DNA. My ancestors were Norwegian, and although I never knew I was living by the Law of Jante, that was evident in the culture I grew up in. The goal of Janteloven is to keep people humble. In their minds, there is a reason most of the tyrannical leaders in history have not come from Scandinavian countries.

The Unchecked Ego

When you look at the great tragedies of the human race, most of them were connected to unchecked egos. This Scandinavian law ensured that no one disrupted the community, and if you did, you were disciplined. You were not thrown in jail, as this is not legislation; but you were ostracized. You were kicked out of the community for appearing "better than" others. You would be socially exiled from family and friends because of your perceived arrogance.

They believe if egos are unchecked, people can take advantage of others. Their organizations follow this same law. It is famously noted that IKEA founder Feodor Ingvar Kamprad, drove a 20-year-old car until he was told it was too dangerous to drive. Unchecked egos can disrupt the plans of a team or organization. People will not want to work with an arrogant person.

One IKEA employee was attempting to load a table into a customer's vehicle. It was not working. No matter how they attempted, this table was not going to fit. So, the employee decided to remove the legs, which was against IKEA policy. This simple act changed the entire business model of IKEA and is the foundation for much of their success today. They learned that their customers love the flat-design concept where everything can fit in their vehicle and they will assemble the furniture at home on their own time. The employee feeling that no one was better than anyone else empowered him to have that conversation with leadership. This is a crucial element of the IKEA culture.

A famous healthcare example was when a woman came into the hospital to have her tonsils removed, and when she woke up, she discovered they had removed her leg below the knee. When this situation was analyzed, five individuals thought something was wrong but did not feel okay in that culture to speak up. The physicians believed they were above the feedback of the nurses and refused to listen.

A culture that is ego-driven will lead to turf wars and backstabbing.

Lliam Gallagher, former lead singer for the band Oasis is famous for his antics. He once said "We are bigger and better than the Beatles, than the Stones, the Who, and the Kinks! Oasis is bigger than Jesus, bigger than rock and roll and bigger than

GOD! We will beat them any bloody day." After this statement, the band suffered a bitter breakup.

This is sad because they made great music. That comment does not define him as a human being, but these types of statements are repelling. He had forgotten that at one point, he was in obscurity and no one knew their band. Now, because of his fame, he acted "better than" everyone else. These types of statements often destroy relationships. Since then, he has done some amazing things and contributed to charity events. Yet, fans feel a sense of loss about the additional music they could have made.

This is why the Law of Jante is still alive and well in our organizations. People will pull against someone who is over confident, not for them. People will want to see this person lose or be removed from the organization. The behavior is repelling, as no one likes to feel inferior. It is difficult to be patient when someone is continually talking about how great they are and how they are the best.

This is an extreme example, but these types of situations happen in organizations every day. Early in my career, I worked with many personalities and some unchecked egos. Because I was struggling with confidence issues, at times, I believed I had great ideas but did not feel okay to speak up. I felt judged and as though my feedback wasn't welcomed. In most organizations, decisions have to be made to make it safe to speak truth without consequences. There is a place for strong leadership; however, if people cannot share their views with leadership, then group think and self-justification will be the norm.

So, in some ways, the Law of Jante is helpful in attempting to curb the enthusiasm of some over confident individuals. However, there are also some major drawbacks.

Suppressed Success

When we are in the process of finding and starting a new job, the prospects are promising. We are excited about the new adventure. Once we start the endeavor, we are often disappointed. The first thing we do is look around to understand how others are behaving. This often informs what we believe to be acceptable behavior. In some areas, this is helpful; in others, it is suffocating. A culture that stifles success will lead to under confident employees, and in turn, underwhelmed customers.

There are unintended consequences of an overly humble culture taken too far. When you cannot be excited about your own success for fear of retaliation, there is a problem. Everyone who attempts to do something great has some healthy drive to be appreciated for that contribution. There are many ways to feel appreciated: a genuine compliment, an award, or simply quality time. Whatever style of appreciation is used, most people enjoy knowing their hard work paid off. If individuals are not allowed to be valued for their contributions, over time, most people settle into status quo.

We all know the dangers of the unchecked ego, but what are the dangers of unreached potential?

You have something amazing to offer your organization, and only you can deliver it. It will take some time to determine what that is and work on mastering that; however, it is absolutely worth the effort.

The challenge is when you break out of your current role; others may attempt to put you back in your previous box. They will ask a question like, "Who do you think you are?" There are many reasons people do not want you to succeed. They could be jealous of your success. They could view you as a threat to a position they want. They could find your newfound success annoying because they liked the previous version of you. Whatever the reasons, this is the Law of Jante at work. The inability to own your greatness also impacts mental health. If you believe you have nothing to offer your organization, what is your purpose in working?

In order to change a culture, it is critical to understand how contributions are valued and egos are kept in check. This is a delicate balance, but it must be achieved for a culture to thrive. If the culture is out of balance, you will either lack progress or a sense of team.

Encouraging some leaders to focus on being a servant is not good advice. Norway is attempting to change their culture right now, with some declaring that the Laws of Jante are dead and Norwegians have to start thinking differently about success. They are now learning that one size does not fit all. Teaching individuals with under confidence to serve more may cause more harm than good. Under confident individuals are already serving, they need to focus on advocating for themselves. On the other hand, Norwegians do not want to become an egocentric culture where everyone is in it for themselves. Changing culture is some of the most difficult work any leader will face.

The key is creating a culture where success is applauded and egos are checked when necessary. In this type of culture, you feel empowered to make a decision, and you are not judged for it. Your effort is celebrated and jealousy is low. Everyone is working hard for a common goal and individual contributions are recognized. The mission of the organization is the highest priority, but it is clearly understood that a team is made up of many individual contributors.

You should feel okay to be bold and strong with your opinions and yet be open to feedback without defensiveness.

Feedback is a gift if you view it as fuel for growth. You know you are making progress when people can disagree with you, and, as a result, the relationship gains in strength.

So how do you develop a healthy culture? The first step is to define the culture you want to create in your team or organization. A healthy culture values humility and working together. It also values individual contribution and celebrating success. It is giving people permission to be great but not act better than others. Building a culture based on serving others is powerful. Also, at times, leaders need to advocate for themselves. There comes a time in every leader's journey when they need to stand up for what they believe.

Healthy cultures guide under confident individuals to find courage and over confident individuals to find humility. Building leaders who build culture is the strategy proven to work.

CHAPTER 4

Authentic Confidence Explained

The **Authentic Confidence Model explains how our confidence issues impact others.** Leaders who communicate with Authentic Confidence build an environment where everyone on the team is comfortable owning their greatness and growth areas. To explain Authentic Confidence, I will be slowing down the communication process using the Authentic Confidence Model.

First, we receive INPUT or feedback. Depending on the feedback, we respond with either over, under, or Authentic Confidence. There are certain personalities or topics that will trigger us to respond with over or under confidence. This is when we are not at our best. It might be based on education, experience, age, gender, background, or the tone of someone's voice. Whatever the reason, triggers cause us to negatively react. A confidence trigger is a vulnerable spot in our career where we are sensitive to feedback. Triggers are comments that create a negative emotional reaction. We create an unhealthy dynamic with others.

One client I worked with was sensitive about his education. When others made comments, he would negatively react and create an awkward environment for the team. He would then storm out of the office and negatively impact how customers viewed him. Once he understood the core issue of this trigger, he was able to develop a strategy to deal with it.

Once we understand our triggers, it is essential to create a game plan to resolve these issues. If we do not, we will cycle between over and under confidence. This is the middle of the model. We'll be blaming others or ourselves for things not working out. We are getting triggered, and we do not know how to productively respond. Authentic Confidence is the process of getting to the root confidence issues, resolving them and responding with the appropriate amount of confidence in every situation. We understand the changes we need to make and have a clear road map to get there. When we start communicating with Authentic Confidence, customers will respond. They want nothing more than to partner with someone they can trust who provides an exceptional experience without drama. This is the OUTPUT portion of the model when we are in control of our emotions and share exactly what we want to share no matter the INPUT.

In order for the model to work, we must resolve our core confidence issues. If we are simply dealing with the symptoms, no meaningful change will occur.

Confidence issues are barriers to career growth. If you do not identify and resolve your core confidence issues, you will be reacting to them your entire career. Once you learn how to resolve one major confidence issue, you will have the blueprint for resolving all of your confidence issues. You will then be able to teach the process to others; this is the highest form of influence.

When the Beatles first formed, all of the members challenged each other in the purest sense. It was about creating great music. It was not about who deserved the credit, or determining the best Beatle. It was about making sure every song that was released measured up to their standard. Each band member had at least one song per album and they pushed each other to reach for something interesting. They were not negatively triggered by feedback; they used it as fuel to propel their music forward.

Imagine an environment where everyone you work with is motivated to produce at the highest levels and work together as a team. Music has the ability to create a unified culture faster than any other medium. Artists join together to create something bigger than themselves. Concerts pull millions of individuals together every day to celebrate with recording artists. Why is that? I was recently at a Garth Brooks concert where over 70,000 people came together to have a great time. The culture was positive, passionate, considerate, sharing, and high energy. There is something about music that unifies us. I can be in a terrible mood, but if my favorite song comes on the radio, instantly, I will be in a great mood, singing along. Unfortunately, for most people, work is not like a concert.

There are many people who remind me of this statement, "It's not supposed to be fun; that's why they call it work."

I am not sure who first coined that phrase, but there is some truth to it. The point of this book is not to tell you that every moment at work is going to be filled with rainbows and unicorns. The fact is, you will do some things at work that will be hard and not fun.

I am not promising that when you find confidence, you will never have a setback or challenge again. The point of this book is this: if you find confidence, you will have the resilience to handle the struggles and mistakes. When you communicate confidence in every situation, you will create a culture in which it is easier to love your work and enjoy your teammates.

All of the positive outcomes start from a genuine care about your work. When you are engaged, you communicate in a way that engages others. This will increase your influence and enhance your results. That is why loving your work is important.

This book will teach you a coaching process to find your Authentic Confidence and love your work. I will provide strategies for working with individuals with over confident and under confident behaviors. This practical approach is the secret to building an unstoppable career and team. I have taught this process to thousands and witnessed the transformation in their careers.

CHAPTER 5

Core Beliefs of an Unstoppable Career

ecording artists mastered the process of moving from obscurity to influence. They accomplished this through identifying and resolving their confidence issues and learning how to communicate with Authentic Confidence. In order to understand how the artists made this transition, it is important to understand their core beliefs. These beliefs provided resilience in their careers when things were difficult and allowed them to remain grounded when they skyrocketed into success.

Authentic Confidence is defined by two Core Beliefs: Pride in Work + Humility in Relationships

Core Belief #1: Pride in Work

Why pride in work?

In my research, I read hundreds of artist autobiographies and biographies. I watched thousands of hours of interviews. When artists were interviewed about an upcoming project, the most common response was, "We are so proud of this new record."

At first, I did not think anything about this statement, but it became so repetitive, I couldn't ignore it. Every artist I respected spoke about their work in the exact same way. They were proud of their work. They believed it made a difference, and they took it very seriously. They did not always take themselves seriously, but they always took the work seriously. The quality of the music mattered.

So, what did this mean to me? They work in an industry called show business and I do not want to be viewed as a showoff. I had an aversion to the idea of pride, yet the phrase was shared so often, I couldn't ignore it. I decided to dig deeper into the statement to see if I were missing something.

The definition of *pride* is "a feeling or deep pleasure or satisfaction derived from one's own achievements, the achievements of those with whom one is closely associated, or from qualities or possessions that are widely admired."

This definition took me by surprise. For a word that is so negatively perceived, the definition appeared to be exactly what I wanted in my career. Why was it that I was having such a hard time with the word *pride?* I think it was because I had heard my whole life that "pride goes before the fall," and no one wants to be viewed as arrogant.

I never wanted to be "that guy" who was full of himself. I knew what unhealthy pride looked like, but could there be a healthy version? To answer this question, I started studying and observing great leaders.

When their team did a great job, the most common statement they would make is, "I am so proud of my team." Then I watched parents. When their child did something remarkable, there was only one response that captured the moment: "I am so proud of you." There is no substitute that works. The research leading to this statement became so overwhelming that I had to apply it to my life, and it became Core Belief #1.

Healthy pride is finding significant satisfaction from your career.

One of the groups who demonstrated Pride in Work is the Irish rock band, U2. They have stood the test of time and are considered one of the greatest bands of all time.

In the early years, life was not easy for U2. They were a politically charged band and received hate mail and even death threats. Prior to one concert, Bono, the lead singer, had received one of these death threats—only this time, authorities believed the threat to be credible. The threat stated that if they played one particular song, Bono would be shot. As the concert drew near, the band's manager and handlers all told them not to play the song. They were told the song was too political and they had plenty of other songs to play.

However, Bono and the band were not just entertainers. They believed their music had the power to change lives. They believed their work mattered, and when the moment arrived, they performed the song. Bono was so nervous during the song that he closed his eyes for the entire performance. As the song concluded and he opened his eyes, he saw his band mate standing in front of him. Evidently, as soon as the song started, the bass player, Adam Clayton, stepped in front of Bono and stood there until the end.

Their music mattered that much to them, and still does.

This is what I missed. My work did not really matter that much. It did not matter if I did a great job or an average job. No one noticed and no one seemed to care. I realized that I needed to care first. If I did not care about the work, no one else would. So, I decided to adopt this belief for myself. From that point forward, my work mattered, and I took pride in it.

Core Belief #2 Humility in Relationships

The second part of the definition of *Authentic Confidence* is humility in relationships. **Healthy humility is taking equal ownership of your greatness and growth areas.** You should believe you are great, but that doesn't make you a better person than others. You may be better at specific skills, but that does not make you a better human being.

To be candid, I studied some recording artists who lacked humility. They believed because they were rock stars, they were superior humans. They had pride in their work, but they did not have humility in relationships. The results were obvious. They experienced broken relationships and lives filled with gossip and drama. The artists I respected were able to avoid this trap. They knew they were great, and they understood humility was needed to develop enduring relationships. It is what held their bands together.

Humility in relationships allows you to work with people for a long time. Artists such as Tom Petty and the Heartbreakers, The Rolling Stones, and U2 were all big hits because of pride in work, but they survived the longest because of humility in relationships.

You may be better at a skill, but that doesn't mean you are a better person. You allow others to take the main stage when it is their turn. You listen without the intent to respond, and you pull for others to do well. You assume the best in others until they prove otherwise, and you are not intimidated or jealous of others' success. You are driven by individual and team accomplishments.

Sir Paul McCartney had his greatest creative output when he was writing hit singles and records with John Lennon. They had a healthy rivalry and pushed each other to make The Beatles one of the greatest rock and roll bands ever.

However, later in their time together as part of the Beatles, they lost humility. Paul and John no longer got along. At the same time, John Lennon was quoted as saying, "We are more popular than Jesus." These "better than" statements are divisive. Words have power, and these over confident statements can destroy relationships and teams.

The irony of this statement is that it came during the last year the Beatles would tour live. They were a studio-only band after that, and they officially broke up in 1970. Public lawsuits and arguments between members continued for years. This is the cost of a lack of humility in relationships.

Thankfully, the story does not end there. Following his success in the Beatles, John recorded some amazing music. He found causes that he believed in deeply. He became an icon with a purpose. It was not about him; it was about how he could help others. This was a beautiful transformation, and when he was suddenly taken from this world, millions grieved losing him.

As I continued to read these stories, I started to have hope. I saw how people of influence can change. Could the pattern they followed apply to me and my life? At first, I was hesitant. I did not want to come off as a showoff. My life had nothing to do with show business, but there was something so authentic about the way these artists created their successes. They had a genuine belief in themselves, and that was contagious and attractive. They knew they had something unique to offer and became experts at delivering the goods. They were not showing off; they were showing up with the best version of themselves. They learned how to conquer their confidence issues and let the world see their originality. This is exactly what I wanted for my career.

I spent the next several years studying this pattern, defining it, trying it out on my own life, and eventually creating a process to share it with others. The pattern is called The 5 Stages of Career Confidence and is covered in Phase III of this book.

It turned my career around. I went from hating my work to loving it. I went from driving laps around my office building because I did not want to go in to showing up every day, ready to make a difference. I have since shared this pattern with thousands of others, and it has been a blast to watch the transformation in their careers.

CHAPTER 6

Growing Your Influence

What can one person do? On April 15th, 2013, a terrorist attack occurred at the Boston Marathon. The world seemed to grieve with Boston as they wondered how the city would react to such a tragedy. Then, one of its favorite sons stepped up to the plate.

April 20th, 2013, David Ortiz, a star player for the Boston Red Sox baseball franchise, known by fans as "Big Papi," took the stage. It was the first time the Red Sox were back to Fenway Park after the attack. Big Papi took the mic and told the fans that the jerseys they wore did not say Red Sox; they said Boston. And he added "Boston is our city! And nobody is going to dictate our freedom! Stay Strong!"

The Red Sox had taken last place in their division the previous year, but Big Papi's speech made it clear he was not living in the past; he was focused on what his team would do this year.

His short speech ignited nothing short of a miracle. From that moment on, the Red Sox had something to prove. They were out to show the world what the city of Boston meant to each player. They were driven, they were united, and they were fearless. The team felt the weight of the situation, and they were going to give their fans something to be excited about.

As the season progressed, they started winning. Many experts and commentators believed Boston could make a run, but no one was predicting what would happen next.

Big Papi kept rallying the troops. Every time he stepped onto the plate, he set an example for the rest of the team. He told the team that nothing mattered as much as this season right now. They may have been baseball players, but they believed their impact was much greater than the game.

They continued to win and even won their division. They moved from last to first—one of the few times in baseball history this had been accomplished. Now, some experts and commentators started paying even more attention to Boston. Could they make a run in the World Series? Could they go from last in their division to World Series Champions? Surely, this emotion would eventually wear off and the team would come back to earth.

In the World Series, they faced a very talented St. Louis Cardinal team, but the momentum and focus of the Boston team proved too much for the opposition. They won the World Series at Fenway Park where Big Papi's speech had been made just months before.

It was the first time since 1918 that Boston won the World Series at Fenway Park. Who was the MVP of the World Series? Of course, it was David Ortiz. The first words in his acceptance speech his were, "This one's for you, Boston. You guys deserve it. We've been through a lot this year and this is for all of you and all the families struggling with the bombing from earlier this year. This is for all of you." His final comment wasn't just for his teammates, but for the city of Boston as well, "Nobody can ever hold us down."

What changed? They believed. They knew they had the ability to bring back the swagger of their city. They went from a team filled with struggle and frustration to a team laser-focused on taking back their city, giving the fans of Boston something to cheer about.

They had a vocal leader who influenced them every day. It was contagious. The message was, "You can hit us, and you may knock us down, but you can't knock us out. You don't know anything about Boston. You don't know who we are and what we stand for. You haven't seen anything yet. You just sit back and watch what we do this year. Sit back and observe the strength of this city."

Ortiz became the spokesman for Boston. He took pride in the work he needed to do for his city. Sometimes, the world is watching and waiting for someone to stand up. They are waiting to follow someone; someone who inspires them, someone who has the courage to lead when times are tough.

David demonstrated Authentic Confidence. What did he gain? Worldwide influence, a huge salary, a championship ring, and, most important, lifetime memories with the team he loved. If you want to love your work, you need to influence others. **Finding and coaching Authentic Confidence is the highest form of influence.**

David Ortiz will be remembered as one of the greatest baseball players of all time; there is no question about that. What I will remember most is the Authentic Confidence that he demonstrated when he walked on the field and said, "This is our city and we are strong."

Big Papi was driven to succeed individually, but his major contribution was to his Red Sox team and the city of Boston. He could have focused on having the best batting average or leading the league in home runs. Instead, he focused on the team winning, and knew he would have to deliver his best in order for that to happen.

When you communicate the appropriate amount of confidence in every situation, you demonstrate the highest form of influence: trust. When your confidence and competence are aligned, you will find significance at work.

When Johnny Marr approached Morrissey to form a band, he had one purpose: produce honest music. The Smiths delivered on that promise. They were a tight four-piece band with Morrissey's lyrics, led by Marr's groundbreaking guitar work. In the next several years, they created four records that are considered some of the most influential of the 1980s. Morrissey explains that when he wrote the lyrics, he meant them. He was not writing to impress anyone; he was writing to share the experiences of life in Manchester. They recorded few music videos because they wanted the music and lyrics to be the focus. They were an authentic band that appeared live. Hundreds of bands have since launched because of the influence of The Smiths.

Once you find Authentic Confidence for yourself, you will inspire others to do the same.

There are four quadrants to understand your journey toward Authentic Confidence.

AUTHENTIC CONFIDENCE QUADRANTS

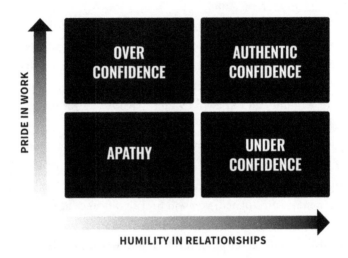

The first quadrant is apathy, which is low pride in work and low humility in relationships. People in the apathy quadrant have the lowest level of influence. They are unable to motivate themselves, thus unequipped to motivate others. They struggle with low ambition and a low sense of urgency. They do not seem to care about anything at work and are floating through their career.

Under confidence is the second quadrant. This person has a low level of pride in work and a high level of humility in relationships. They influence relationships, but often struggle influencing the results. They struggle making the tough calls necessary to deliver an exceptional customer experience. They may spend time managing perceptions and worrying about others' opinions of them. They have difficulty making decisions and do not believe their work is that important. They often deflect compliments and do not allow others to validate their work.

The third quadrant is over confidence. This is where pride in work is high, and humility in relationships is low. They have strong influence around results, but often lack the ability to influence relationships. In other words, the person believes the numbers matter most. They spend more time speaking than listening. They believe they have the best ideas in the room and can do everyone's job better than they do. The goal is to get the title, the money, and the recognition. No one lives up to their expectations.

The final quadrant is Authentic Confidence. This person takes great pride in their work and has humility in relationships. They are gifted influencers for both relationships and results. They have the most productive teams, creating the greatest customer experience. They see the value in their contribution and the importance of their work. They understand the value of strong relationships and have an accurate view of themselves and others. They are introspective and understand their greatest strengths as well as their most significant growth areas. They are refreshing to be around and quick to share the glory with the team. They are honest optimists in action.

The importance of creating influencers has never been more important. Why is influence so important? Is it easy for your competition to steal your marketing? They can follow your efforts and say all of the same things. Is it easy for your competition to steal your talent? If you are building an organization of influencers, the answer will be NO. They will not be able to recruit your talent away if your organization is filled with great leaders. Everyone wants to work for a great leader, yet not everyone is willing to go through the effort to become one.

Influencers have the ability to withstand all types of adversity. When others join the organization, the influencers will determine whether that new person will stay or leave, shrivel or thrive. When you create an intentional leadership development system based on excellence and not perfection, influencers will devour it. Individuals want to grow and work for teams who are growing. There is a healthy swagger that influencers bring to a culture. These influencers will create a powerhouse without competitors. No one can copy that formula. Your talent growing in influence is your greatest competitive advantage. Once you are filled with influencers, you can move forward with effective strategies.

Unfortunately, in most cultures, talking about confidence issues is not appropriate. Everyone is doing their job, but the elephants in the room are not discussed. So, you have people with unchecked egos running amuck. They may be producing extraordinary results, but no one wants to work with them.

On the other end of the spectrum, you have capable and talented individuals waiting in the wings to make a contribution, but they do not feel okay doing so. They do not believe it is their place to speak up or offer a new way of doing things. This belief is a confidence killer. When people have contributions to make but they are not making them, your customers are losing out on the very opportunities that could be game changers for your organization. We must provide a path for people to grow their influence. It is not about becoming the expert in everything. It is about knowing your authentic contribution, sharing it, and valuing the unique contribution of others.

Sir Edmond Hillary was a New Zealand climber and part of the British expedition to ascend Mount Everest in 1953. In the 1940s and 1950s, climbing Mount Everest was seen as an issue of country pride. Who would be the first to ascend Mount Everest and live to talk about it? Teams from France, Switzerland, Britain, and many other nations raced to be the first.

Historically, expeditions treated the local climbers, called Sherpas, as servants. They were not seen as equals or peers until the 1953 expedition when Sir Edmond Hillary changed everything. He cared about the Sherpas. He took care of them as if they were his own team. He even made a Sherpa his climbing partner.

Tenzig Norgay would be Hillary's closest teammate on the route. It was a brutal climb, but eventually, Sir Edmond Hillary and Tenzig Norgay made it to the top and safely back down.

On their return to base camp, everyone wanted to know who first stepped on the top of mighty Mount Everest. Sir Edmond Hillary stated that he and Tenzig Norgay stepped on the peak together.

The journalists needed to write one name in the record books, however, so they pressed for a name. Was it Hillary or Norgay? Edmund refused to answer. He said they climbed Everest together and it would be the British and Sherpas who would be listed in the record books. The story remained for ten years until Tenzig finally let it slip that Edmund first stepped on the summit. The first call he received was from Edmund, letting Tenzig know that he believes they made it together. No matter what the media reported, in his mind, they ascended Everest together. Edmond believed he could not have done it alone, and he honored his friend Tenzig until his death. Edmund had pride in his work, demonstrated humility, and that led him to influence.

Phase II: Self-Assessment

Increase Your Self-Awareness

CHAPTER 7

The Biology of Confidence

reat leaders communicate the appropriate amount of confidence in every situation. How do we find that balance between over confidence and under confidence? It starts with understanding our confidence tendencies. Many of our confidence issues are connected to our DNA. The University of California Los Angeles has researched our genetic predisposition to certain levels of self-esteem. The oxytocin receptor gene has been found to predict whether someone has a bias toward optimism or low self-esteem. The research is available in the online edition of the journal *Proceedings of the National Academy of Sciences (PNAS)* and in the journal's September 13, 2011 print edition.

In other words, we are biologically hard-wired with a tendency to lean toward one end of the confidence continuum. This is why Authentic Confidence is challenging; it is not a natural state. Each of us has a bias. That does not mean we are stuck in that bias, but rather, we have to learn how to overcome the bias.

No matter how you were raised, your biology favors either the glass half-full or half-empty. For example, some people are able to quickly get over things and move on while others have a difficult time; it is based on a biological disposition.

If you struggle advocating for yourself or believing you are ready for the next challenge, you may have a biological bias toward under confidence. If you have noticed that you exaggerate your skills to others and have seen your confidence outpace your competence, then you may have a biological bias toward over confidence. The good news is that your genetics define your starting point, not your ending point. No matter your bias, you can work toward finding that sweet spot for your own leadership. When you find that sweet spot, you will be living the core beliefs of Pride in Work + Humility in Relationships. One of the ways to consider your bias toward over or under confidence is to examine compliments and criticisms.

Compliments

When someone offers you a compliment, how do you respond? If you do not respond well you may struggle with under confidence.

If you respond well, you will demonstrate pride in your work and gain influence. If you do not handle compliments well—for example, when someone gives you a compliment, and you deflect it—people will lose trust in you. The person giving you the compliment will walk away feeling disappointed. The giver is attempting to validate all your hard work and wants a mutually beneficial exchange. Instead, they feel disconnected and frustrated that you did not accept the encouragement.

What is the root cause? Bragophobia—the fear of looking like a bragger. No one wants to be seen as boastful, so we go to great lengths to avoid that reputation. The unintended consequences of bragophobia is under confidence. We make sure no one thinks we are over confident, so we undersell our capabilities. We view this as humility; however, taken too far, we no longer advocate for ourselves or accept compliments.

At a young age, I saw a bully on the playground. I vowed to never be like that person. I never wanted to be the kid who everyone thought was a "show off." The way I accomplished this was to diminish compliments. When someone said, "great job," I would say some version of, "no big deal." I thought others would view me as humble for not accepting the compliment. That is not what happened.

People want you to accept the compliment with a simple, "Thank you," and when you do not, you are not taking pride in your work. This is a maladaptive strategy that starts from wanting to appear humble and ends up as false humility. False humility is when you know you are good at something yet deny that fact in front of others. It leaves others feeling frustrated in the exchange.

For many years, I responded in this way. For example, if someone thanked me for a great coaching session, I used to deflect it. A mentor of mine finally said, "knock it off." I was confused and a little thrown by the comment. He continued, "You spent hours working with that person and it went well; own it."

He was right and the same is true for you. When you do a great job, own it! It is not bragging to say a genuine, "Thank you."

There is a reason why taking pride in your work is the first core belief. It is the start of Authentic Confidence. **If you are willing to genuinely accept a compliment and take pride in your work, you will be on your way to building the career you deserve.**

You will leave the conversation feeling valued and encouraged. This is exactly what the other person wants you to feel. It is a beautiful and collaborative connection, when done properly. When we accept compliments, our teammates will start responding the same way.

I coach so many leaders who will explain how a compliment should be received but will not accept a compliment. They will say to me, "I'm not good at accepting compliments, but I'm great at giving them." This is unfortunate, because actions speak louder than words. If they do not model accepting compliments, eventually, the team will follow the leader. They will eventually stop accepting them as well. Taking pride in your work and accepting compliments will give everyone around you the permission to do the same.

Criticism

How do you handle constructive criticism? If you do not accept any negative feedback from others, you may struggle with over confidence. When you respond well to criticism, you demonstrate humility in relationships. You will gain influence and others will feel safe talking with you about your strengths and growth areas.

Why is it so hard to hear negative feedback? There are often two reasons. First, you don't believe it is true and you are fighting back. Secondly, you believe it is true, but you don't like someone rubbing it in your face. Either way, it is easy to overreact or underreact. When our reaction is not appropriate to the feedback, trust is lost.

The Authentic Confidence model, at the beginning of the book explains feedback responses. Some people hear feedback and move into over confidence. When they hear negative feedback, they will say things like, "I totally disagree with you," "You never trained me to do that," "I never knew about that deadline," or "Why aren't you talking to the rest of the team? They're the problem." These defensive responses demonstrate blame of self or others. These statements, if unaddressed, will lead to dysfunctional teams where feedback is not given or received.

The reason why these responses are so common is because criticism challenges our identity. If we believe we are great employees, this criticism challenges that belief. Someone is saying we are not great and that there is something wrong with us.

So, what do we do? We defend ourselves. We stand up for ourselves and share our side of the story. This served us well early in life. If we were blamed for eating the last cookie, and did not do it, we wouldn't roll over and take the blame. The problem occurred when we did eat the last cookie and denied it. That lack of honesty infuriates others. It leads to denial.

There are many reasons why people live in denial. They may have had a parent or sibling who told them they would never measure up.

Many individuals who demonstrate over confidence are masking their under confidence. A common strategy to deal with rejection is to reject others first. Defensiveness is a reflex and they surround themselves with people who agree with them. Any disagreement is seen as an attack and will not be tolerated.

If we will not accept any feedback, others become increasingly frustrated with us. They will no longer offer feedback because they know we will not listen. So they give up on us and the relationship breaks down. They take their comments underground because sharing them is not safe.

Unfortunately, much of this stems from under confidence. If we do not feel good about ourselves, we may have a fear that the criticism is true and we really do not measure up.

If we feel unworthy in our new position and believe we are imposters, we will struggle with difficult feedback. We are already anxious about being found out as incompetent, so we work hard to prove others wrong instead. We want to prove we can do it and that we are the right person for the job.

If we are completely honest, however, we are not sure we are the best person for the job. We are still trying to prove we are the right person to ourselves, and this can create a level of paranoia. We are worried about what others are thinking of us. We quickly discount criticism. The problem is when we discount criticism, it simply goes underground, and it will turn into gossip.

This is why the first step is taking pride in our work. Once you have pride in your work and you know why you are valued at work, it will allow you to handle the criticism. It is the understanding that feedback is not to be avoided; it is a gift to help you improve.

When we own the fact that we are not perfect and have work to do, we become open to the idea of feedback. There are still right and wrong ways to give it, but, at least, we are open to hearing it. It allows us to take ownership of feedback that is appropriate and ditch the rest.

It does not mean you accept everything at face value, but it also does not mean you reject it all without reflection. Honor the person giving you the feedback, evaluate what you are hearing, and share it with someone you trust. Accept what is appropriate and reject the rest. This is how you will respond when you are responding to feedback with Authentic Confidence. When you hear negative feedback, thank the person for bringing it to your attention. Ask humble questions to ensure you are clear, and give them a timeline to reflect and respond. Follow up with a meaningful conversation. The goal is not to eliminate negative feedback, but to learn from it.

Your ability to appropriately respond to feedback is largely based on your self-awareness. Self-awareness is having an accurate view of yourself and being equally comfortable with your greatness and weakness. If you do not have an accurate view of yourself, you may ask for help when you do not need it or offering help that is not valuable. Arrogance and insecurity often create a misalignment between confidence and competence.

Effective leaders know when to ask for help and when to provide it. They have the ability to handle all sorts of feedback and to respond with confidence.

If self-awareness is essential to effective leadership, how do you increase it? The first step is to align your confidence and competence. In other words, it is the ability to honestly evaluate the quality of your work and relationships. Unstoppable careers start with an honest view of how good you are and how you talk about it. The Phase II Self-Assessment will help you understand your current level of confidence. In Phase III, you will learn the secrets to grow your competence.

CHAPTER 8

Confidence Profile: Peace Keeper

A confidence continuum exists, and we are all on it. In order to understand our confidence tendencies, it is important to take an honest self-evaluation. This will increase self-awareness.

Self-awareness is critical in leadership and is the first step in working through your confidence challenges. Self-assessments are safe pathways for you to take an honest look in the mirror. When it comes to confidence issues, labels are dangerous. Calling someone arrogant or insecure is a sure way to shut down a conversation.

After thousands of coaching sessions around confidence challenges, I discovered all of the participants fell into one of six profiles. These profiles represent our confidence tendencies and help us understand how to best interact with others. The

Confidence Profiles are Peace Keeper, Friend Maker, Inquisitor, Negotiator, Driver, and Convincer. There is no right or wrong profile, as leadership is about progress not perfection. One of the greatest myths regarding confidence issues is that people are in a fixed state. People believe that some individuals are over confident and others are under confident in all areas of life. Some people fit in this category, but this is the exception, not the rule. We all have a bias toward over or under confidence, but this is not a fixed state; it is a tendency.

Whatever your profile, you will learn the ability to connect to the other profiles and elevate your level of influence. The Confidence Profiles were created to be used as a starting point for your career development, not the ending point.

CONFIDENCE PROFILES

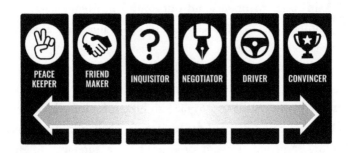

Each of the profiles has a set of characteristics. You have a primary Confidence Profile at work that guides the way you view communication, conflict, and change. If you are interested in taking the Confidence Profile Assessment, visit BenFauske. com. The following is an explanation of each profile.

Confidence Profile: Peace Keeper

Taylor is a Peace Keeper and almost everyone likes her. She works hard at what she does and does not want to let anyone down. She takes on the tasks that others avoid and spends time supporting others. She prides herself in being relaxed and does not like high stress. She believes that the most successful leaders and teams have low drama.

Taylor does not like conflict for the sake of conflict and is uncomfortable with awkward conversations. When others are too aggressive, she will retreat. She is humble and has a hard time with people who do not share her values. She is prone to judging others who are self-serving or act superior. She does not enjoy criticism, as she is often her own harshest critic. She keeps to herself, but when she gives a compliment, it is genuine. She is looking for mutually beneficial relationships, but, sometimes, others can take advantage of her. She does not want the spotlight, and if she chooses the spotlight, it is because she has done the work necessary to be prepared.

She wants to be included and has found one of the best ways to be included is to serve. She pays attention to the details and will notice the small things people need. She struggles with stress at times and does not feel she has permission to really speak her mind. She is not sure if her opinion is correct, or even if it matters. She is looking for ways to fit in and wants to be in the background more than out front. She would prefer hanging out with a select few instead of a large group of people.

She is motivated by how things will improve. She likes a fair warning on changes and does not respond well to being pushed. She will often not push back, but she will be resentful of the person pushing. She will view that person as demanding and aggressive. She will move forward, but not because of false urgency or moving for the sake of moving. She wants to have a conversation about the change. Once she clearly understands the benefits of the change, she will be a loyal advocate for the change. If she does not have time to assimilate the information and is just expected to get on board quickly, she will comply, but she will not be invested in the process. This can lead to disengagement and blaming others for a dysfunctional workplace.

Top Value

Peace Keepers are looking for moments of calm.

Ideal Environment

They are at their best in relaxed and productive environments.

Strengths

Peace Keepers create relaxing environments. They leave room for others to contribute to ideas. They listen without the intent to respond; they seek to understand. They can make others feel important. They create calm out of chaos and will help others slow down and take a breath. They are dependable and enjoy routine and rhythm. They understand the value of planning and being prepared. They will form strong and trusting relationships and will produce steady results.

They value having some margin time and will ask questions like, "Do we always need to be in a panic mode?" or "Must we always have to run at this pace?" They believe the best leaders take time to reflect in order to create an effective plan. Thoughtful leadership leads to effective decision making. Peace Keepers bring this slowing of the pace. It does not mean they do not work hard; it means they value a quiet contemplative style, and, although it is often discounted, they know the value that space provides.

Growth Areas

Peace Keepers may struggle advocating for themselves and others may fill the vacuum left by inaction. They may become overly excited during stressful situations. It will be hard for them to shake off mistakes. They may struggle blaming themselves or others for problems. They tend to avoid conflict even if it is necessary. They may take their work too seriously and need a large amount of time to complete certain tasks. They may not handle change well and want to stay with the status quo. They will need to understand clearly how life will be better in the future before they buy into the change. They may allow relational issues to linger. They may feel uncomfortable being the center of attention or speaking in public. They know what they do not want but may not know what they want.

When it is time to move an initiative forward, and they do not have the clear picture, they will struggle with their internal monologue. They will think things like, *Maybe I'm not good enough to pull this off, Do we have to do this?* or *What would happen if I just didn't do it and avoided the whole situation?* They will struggle withholding judgment from those who push. They do not like to be forced into anything. They do not enjoy the peer pressure and do not feel the same rush from a crazy-paced work environment. They want to be productive and useful but believe life is meant to be enjoyed in the moments and not just at the mountain tops.

Motivations

When working with a Peace Keeper, it is important to remember they are often flexible with their ideas. They will never tell others what to do, and they do not like being told what to do. They are typically great with customers and have a high empathy for others. They want to make sure others approve of their decisions, and they treat everyone fairly. They will often look for ways to reduce the tension when it is too high.

They see the value of people feeling safe and creating a judgment-free work environment. They believe too much stress can be counterproductive. Everyone knowing what is expected of them, and building a routine to achieve the results is ideal.

Interactions

Peace Keepers are looking for common ground. They want space in conversations for each person to share. They resist aggression and want to consider all options. They will likely not fight back if they disagree with your position. Watch for subtle signs of disagreement and ask their opinion without judgment. If they feel judged about their perspective, they will stop sharing. Don't assume you know what they are thinking. Ask open-ended questions and take the time to listen. You will often be surprised at what you hear.

Clear expectations will allow them to feel more comfortable, as it will reduce surprises. They will not often question authority and will seek compromise in solutions. There needs to be alignment with the pace of change. They are sensitive to increased urgency and will view it as unnecessary stress if not properly explained. Once they understand the reasons for the change, they will create a plan to make it happen.

Conflict and Change

Peace Keepers work best at a steady and comfortable pace. They want you to appreciate their space and take the time to understand their perspective. They want room to contribute to the conversation, but will not force their way in. They want to feel included and appreciated. They do not want to take charge and will allow you to lead if you take time to understand their perspective. They want to know you like them and value their efforts. They want to know the relationship is stable and criticism will be handled in a calm conversation. They will shut down if you are too aggressive. They know the work must be done and can handle tough feedback if you are kind. They do not want to be rushed or coerced into decisions or change. If they are upset, they will often communicate their frustrations indirectly. Watch for subtle comments of disagreement or changes in body language.

Peace Keepers are loyal and giving. They are sensitive to your comments, so choose your words wisely. They will work hard to make sure you are happy with the results. They will avoid unnecessary drama and may be uncomfortable with gossip, so watch for cues that they are disconnected from the conversation. They desire a stress-free work environment and, although they know that is unlikely, they will work hard to create it. A productive day with low distractions will be ideal.

CHAPTER 9

Confidence Profile: Friend Maker

Cheri is a Friend Maker. When she is at work, she does not want anyone to be left behind. She will make new employees feel welcome and invite them into conversations. She looks for the individuals who are left out and finds ways to include them. She does not pity these individuals; she simply has empathy for them. She has the ability to sense what the underdog is feeling and hates it when others are excluded. She is warm and friendly to everyone she meets. She is looking for connections and ways to encourage the other person. She finds great joy in seeing others thrive. She is not jealous of others but celebrates their successes.

She is uncomfortable with conflict and will look for ways to avoid it. This can cause her to be resentful of situations that do not go her way. She will not address the issue immediately, which will cause her to stir, and she may eventually erupt. If she feels she is disrespected or not treated fairly, she will react strongly. She is also uncomfortable being in the spotlight. She is comfortable giving compliments but is suspicious when receiving them. She would prefer making things happen in the background and will look for ways to serve others. She is great with customers and will go the extra mile to ensure people have what they need to be successful. She knows what she does not want but often is not clear about what she wants. She will advocate for others, especially those less fortunate, far more than she will advocate for herself. She is often sensitive to the comments of others. She is cordial in most situations, and that is what she expects from others. She knows conflict needs to happen at times, but she does not look for it.

Top Value

Friend Makers are looking for moments of genuine connection.

Ideal Environment

Friend Makers are at their best when they enjoy the people they are working with.

Strengths

Friend Makers make others feel welcome and included. When they first meet someone, they want to form a connection. They want to be liked and want to demonstrate they like others. They look for common ground and ways to reduce stress and anxiety. They prefer to live in a state of calm. They want people to do things the right way. They believe you should treat people the way they want to be treated. They tend to be more interested in relationships than results. They believe the results will work out as long as the relationships are working.

Friend Makers look for ways to build rapport with others and are great team players. They work hard to ensure the results are achieved and are great with customers. They have high empathy for others, especially others who are like-minded. They will stick up for the underdog or those who struggle defending themselves. They are quick to encourage others and will often send thank you notes and gifts that demonstrate appreciation.

Growth Areas

They will have a hard time defining what they want and advocating for themselves. Friend Makers may become agitated when relationships are not working. They may have a low empathy for those who are not "good friends" or pushy. They demand respect and expect others to give it, and when they don't, they will negatively react. Others have the ability to manipulate them as they can be heavily influenced by other opinions. If someone gossips about another person, it will have an impact on their perception. They love people, but some people annoy them. It is hard for them to calm down once someone has agitated them.

Friend Makers can be stubborn and unsupportive. They understand the power of friendship and can withdraw their emotion when they are not feeling appreciated. They will often use silence to cool off a relationship with others, and this may appear as a passive-aggressive approach. This is how Friend Makers take charge in working relationships, and others may feel isolated and cut off. Because they make very few mistakes at work and work hard to maintain a high level of excellence, others who do not measure up are judged but often not confronted.

Motivations

They are motivated when they have the ability to form strong bonds at work. They thrive in an environment where everyone helps each other. Everyone's contribution is valued, and they feel appreciated for their work. They enjoy others setting clear, logical, and effective strategies to follow. They enjoy knowing their role and what is expected of them and delivering on that every day. They do not like to be pushed or forced to have difficult conversations that are outside their scope of influence. They thrive in environments where everyone gets along.

Interactions

Friend Makers want to laugh and enjoy conversations. They enjoy divergent points of view and do not want to feel judged. They do not work well with bullies. No one does, but Friend Makers will be especially sensitive to those behaviors. If a Friend Maker feels someone is pushing too hard, they will become defensive. They do not like being told what to do, especially if they disagree. They will often not state their frustrations because they do not feel safe.

If they are brought along for the journey and understand where things are heading, they will be supportive. They will think through the relational disconnects that others may not. They want to be treated fairly and expect the same for everyone else. The rules matter and are put in place for a reason.

Conflict and Change

Friend Makers thrive on relationships based on trust. They have high expectations of friends and may desire perfection. If they are frustrated with their friendships, they may not confront the situation directly. They may share the situation with others to seek a different perspective and find clarity. If you have a conflict to share with them, ensure you establish the importance of the relationship. They want to know you care and are sharing this information for their benefit. They may be defensive with the feedback, but if you are consistent and kind, they will reflect on the feedback and make changes.

If their relationships are not working, they will become restless. It is important to provide specific examples calmly and concisely. Allow them time to process the information and come back to you with potential solutions. They do not do well being forced into decisions quickly. They may become resentful if they feel the conversation was too aggressive or one-sided. You will need to continually ask for their side of the story. This conversation will help them process the discussion and prepare for change.

They desire time for personal discussions about family and friends. They want to know how people are doing and not just at the superficial level. They have empathy for others and will strongly support their work friends. They have great insights and enjoy discussing what needs to be done to make the team more effective. They will often withhold suggestions until they are asked, as they do not want to initiate conflict. If you ask their perspective, they will offer it along with potential solutions. They will continue to offer you feedback if you handle it well. If they feel you mishandle the feedback, they will stop providing it. They want you to be fair and consistent in all your interactions.

CHAPTER 10

Confidence Profile: Inquisitor

Jack is an Inquisitor. He questions things he does not understand and loves learning. When he is locked into a project, he will work hard and follow the process. When he does not understand the vision, he will struggle. He is kind and giving and wants friends but wants to understand why people do what they do. He is often confused by behaviors of others and, at times, feels misunderstood.

He can play the role of an instigator but will not typically introduce a direct conflict. If someone else brings up an issue, he will not be afraid to engage it. He prefers peace and quiet to chaos but has the ability to create chaos if needed. He tends to play both sides of an issue just to create some excitement in the conversation. When he does not understand why something is happening, especially to him, he may become stubborn and strong willed. He wants to make sure if something is happening to him, he understands the benefits and deficits. Once he understands, he will be compassionate and fair; when he does not understand, he may appear like he is blocking progress.

He wants to be included in the decision-making process, but he may not have all of the answers. He may slow down the process, not because he wants to be an obstacle but because he wants to make sure all of the details of a decision are considered. He does not always have a clear picture of what he wants, and he wants to figure out the path for himself. Once he has clarity on his direction, he will be steady in pursuing and advocating for that option.

Top Value

Inquisitors are looking for moments of clarity.

Ideal Environment

Inquisitor's ideal environment is where ideas are debated before decisions are made.

Strengths

Inquisitors will be tenacious at understanding the implications of a decision and will not stop asking until they have a clear understanding. They do not prefer conflict but will address it when necessary. They will be open to other ideas and will flex their plan to the other person's perspective if it makes sense. They will become loyal once they understand and buy in to the solution. They are comfortable sharing their feedback. They are interested in change if it leads to improvements. They are looking for opportunities to learn new skills. They are open to joining critical conversations and like to be involved in the decision-making process. They are willing to ask the awkward question to seek clarity. They understand those who are hard charging as well as those who are uncomfortable with change.

They love to challenge the status quo and find better ways of doing things. They will question almost everything, most often, in a respectful and curious way. They do not ask questions they already know the answers to; they find that disrespectful. They ask questions they genuinely want to know the answers to and will continue to ask until they understand. They will be extremely supportive followers when they understand the game plan and will not feel the need to stand up and take charge. If things are going well, they will follow. If things are not going well, they will challenge.

Growth Areas

If they are not on board with a solution, they may appear stubborn and second-guess the strategy. Inquisitors do not respond well to the old parenting technique "Because I said so." They will ask the difficult questions because if they are going to get behind something, they need to know it is legit. They are comfortable in the waiting zone until the correct solution is found. They want to discuss options; they want to visualize how this will work for them, and if they cannot visualize it working, they will silently boycott or stall progress. If they do not agree with a decision, they may argue or withdraw support. They can blame leaders for not disclosing all of the necessary information. They can quit on ideas or projects when they are not working. It may be perceived that they will not move on until they know the answer to the question, "What's in it for me?" They can struggle with relationships because of their continual questioning and challenging.

It may appear they know exactly what they want and are moving toward that direction, but that is often misleading. They are often unclear on their own future. Once they are clear on what they want, they will ask fewer questions and will be ready to get things done. However, when they are not clear, they may appear to question everything. They will find many ways to ask the same sorts of questions. They may derail conversations, as they are curious about many things, and will move conversations in directions that may not serve the purpose of the meeting.

Motivations

Once they are on board and enjoy the solution, they will be loyal and support it with a great attitude. They will get excited about it and will find ways to make the project even more successful. They are comfortable playing a role behind the scenes and will take the stage if needed. They view their questioning as seeking clarity and benefiting everyone involved.

Interactions

Inquisitors can be fun to work with and they can also be frustrating. They will ask the tough questions that others are afraid to ask; however, they may ask these types of questions to a fault. Continually asking questions no one knows the answers to can simply derail a meeting. Those who have a clear direction may feel the Inquisitors are creating conflict for the sake of conflict.

They will have a high empathy for the other five profiles. They understand the need to get things done and the need for calm. The challenge they will face is they do not know how to reconcile those differing opinions. They do not necessarily bring people together; they may instigate conversations that can break groups apart. This is great fun for a team that has a strong foundation, but it can be extremely disruptive to a new or forming team.

The best way to interact with an Inquisitor is to ask them questions to find out their stance. They may be confused about the direction, and seeking their input will help them buy-in to the final solution.

Conflict and Change

Inquisitors want you to answer the question "Why?" Before any crucial conversation happens, they want to know the purpose behind the discussion. If they do not know the reason, they may be uncomfortable and less effective. You will want to explain why you are meeting and your desired outcomes. This will allow them to lower their defenses and join a productive conversation. They thrive on the back story and are comfortable with the gossip or drama that surrounds the situation. They enjoy putting the puzzle pieces together and want to feel like a partner with you.

Inquisitors will advocate change if they understand the personal implications. If they do not understand, they can be barriers to change. If they do not feel included, they will create their own explanation, and it is often not reality. They may tend to gossip about the change and can get caught up in conspiracy theories. They will want to know you are not out to get them. They want to have a direct conversation about what is happening. If they feel details are left out, they may be suspicious about your intentions. In order to help alleviate unnecessary stress, it is important to clearly communicate how this change will impact their position. Once they understand the changes to their role and agree on the direction, Inquisitors will be supportive.

CHAPTER 11

Confidence Profile: Negotiator

Rusty is a Negotiator. He knows what it takes to accomplish the task at hand. He is comfortable with compromise and knows that is needed to get the deal done. He will be quick to partner with others if he thinks it will improve the outcome. He does not feel the need to win at others' expense. He believes there is more than enough room for everyone to succeed. He has his own agenda of what needs to happen for him to be successful. He has developed strong relationships and knows what they want. He is very observant of the words, body language, and the habits of his customers. It is his job to notice these things and he will ask questions to understand their motivations. Once he understands those motivations, he will find solutions to satisfy their needs. He knows that if his customers are happy, he will be successful. Their success will drive his success. He will introduce conflict if there are issues holding back progress.

He will initiate projects to be done and will work hard to ensure the projects are staying on task. When he leaves work at the end of the day, he will think back through his interactions. If his day was filled with successful interactions, he deems that as a successful day. If he simply knocked out a couple of the tasks without meaningful interactions, it will not be deemed a successful day. He is driven by both results and relationships and understands the necessary balance of both.

He is growing in his ability to listen without the intent to respond. He is loyal to his friends and will find ways to value and support others in the organization. He has the ability to see both sides of situations. He knows what he wants and is open to what others want. He prides himself on the ability to find a solution that works for everyone. He will take the time to listen to other perspectives before making a decision. He works hard to find a compromise and a solution that will work best for all parties involved. He is flexible when he needs to be and is firm when required. He will not sacrifice the relationship to get the deal done. He will wait until he finds a workable solution. He believes compromise is a key attribute in successful relationships. He is willing to sacrifice his own needs for the betterment of the team.

Top Value

Negotiators are looking for moments of agreement.

Ideal Environment

A Negotiators ideal environment balances the need for results and relationships.

Strengths

They will still make sure their needs are eventually met, but they are willing to be patient in that effort. They perform well in the toughest situations because they do not overreact to the situation. They are willing to have tough conversations when needed to ensure the project is successful, but they will not generate unnecessary drama. They will be assertive when necessary but will be kind and supportive to teammates most of the time. Only when absolutely necessary will they push an issue.

They have a clear vision of success but are open to listening to other ideas to find a better way. They have a high empathy for other perspectives and know winning together is better. They know that at times, someone needs to make the decision and go, but that is often a last resort. They will seek input from many sources to determine the best course of action. They know the result needed and also the relationships needed to pull off the project. They will have strong relationships in the organization.

Growth Areas

It can often take longer than expected to get the results they are looking for. Some members of the team will want Negotiators to move faster. They may spend too much time gathering support and not enough time moving things forward. They can lose clarity when they have too much group think. It may be difficult to balance those who believe they are moving too slow with those who believe they are moving too fast. If there are strong dissenting views, they may feel stuck. They may become frustrated with those who refuse to get on board, no matter how many conversations they have. Keeping everyone happy can be exhausting. They are in constant tension between getting things done and getting along.

When there are strong conflicts, Negotiators will have a hard time finding a solution. They want everyone to get what they want, and when that is unrealistic, they will struggle with the win/lose proposition. They do not enjoy solutions that leave others feeling frustrated. They want a solution that works best for everyone.

Motivations

They are motivated by getting deals done, finding agreement, and walking forward in lock step. They work well with others and enjoy working on a solution together. A Negotiator often knows the best way to get things done with the support of others. They will work hard and sacrifice much to get what they want. They strongly agree with the win/win philosophy of leadership and believe that they will achieve great success together. They are motivated by getting the deal done. They typically do not work against others; they prefer to work with others so everyone on the team can be successful.

Interactions

Negotiators do a great job at building consensus; however, they are not afraid to advocate for themselves when needed. If others are attempting to derail the plan, the Negotiators may become more assertive and take over. This is not their first approach, but used if necessary. They understand the perspectives of the others and can empathize with each person. They will be patient with their agenda, and they understand, sometimes, a project will take many twists and turns before it is successfully implemented. They are in for the long haul and are willing to sacrifice personal comfort for long-term gains.

When interacting with a Negotiator, it is often best to find out what they want. Their willingness to share their picture of success is often an indicator of the level of trust in the relationship. Remember, when a Negotiator shows their cards, they are in a place of vulnerability. If they tell you something in confidence, and you betray that trust, they will often find ways to work around you in the future. If you maintain confidentiality, the Negotiators will bring you into their thought-making process and allow you input into the direction of things.

Conflict and Change

When working with a Negotiator, they want to know how your discussion is going to help them. They are continually looking for ways to work smarter, faster, and better with others. You can be fairly direct with Negotiators when dealing with change or conflict. They are interested in your perspective. They are continually gathering information to ensure they are using the most effective approach.

They are open to change if they understand how it will help the organization as well as their own success. If the change does not support their success, they will be resistant and will find alternative solutions. They will debate and revisit issues until they find something that works best for everyone. They understand the importance of strong relationships in the context of getting work done. They want to feel like collaborators in solving complicated problems. They know what they want, and they are open to your feedback. They will adjust their plans if you provide a persuasive argument. If they understand the benefits to the project and people, they will be invested in the solution.

CHAPTER 12

Confidence Profile: Driver

Vanessa is a **Driver** and believes her responsibility is to push. She knows that in order to get the best out of people, sometimes you have to push them beyond their comfort zone. She is comfortable being in charge and is often uncomfortable following others. She has a low tolerance for leaders who are not effective. She is comfortable addressing conflict head on, and if someone is not delivering on their promises, she will seek clarity. Once she knows where someone needs to improve, she will be kind but clear about what she expects that person to do. She delivers this feedback for the person's own good. She knows what she wants, and she goes for it. She will ensure she has the support to make it happen, but she gathers support quickly and keeps moving.

She has been successful implementing her ideas in the past and is often convinced she has the right idea for the moment. She has a clear picture of success and believes her role is to convince others that her way is the best way. She is willing to listen to other perspectives but is hesitant to change her mind, as her way is often the best way. She likes getting results and is a goal setter. She knows what she wants and is willing to put in the effort to make that happen. She is primarily focused on her own needs and then will look at the needs of others. She believes that she has great advice, and others would do well to implement her ideas.

Vanessa believes the purpose of work is to make things happen and getting to the top of the mountain is worth the effort. She will briefly celebrate when she gets there, but then she will be ready to take on the next mountain. This is the rush that motivates her to accomplish the next step. She is not interested in participation ribbons; she wants championship trophies.

Top Value

The Driver is passionate about progress.

Ideal Environment

Drivers work best in fast-moving and results-oriented environments.

Strengths

They are hard charging and fast moving. They are results oriented and love to see things move and grow. They are most interested in personally succeeding. They are driven by large challenges. They are constantly looking for ways to improve and keep things moving. They are willing and comfortable addressing the issues that will stall progress. They anticipate issues before they happen and create an internal game plan to address the issues. They are driven by serving customers and ensuring they have what they need. They understand customers are the lifeblood of success.

They are willing to work hard and put in the effort to be successful. They will ignite situations with energy and ideas for forward progress. They have a clear picture of success and are willing to listen to others' ideas as long as they are furthering the project. They are great followers when they are completely aligned with the plan of the project. They will build relationships quickly and will set strong expectations for those on the team. When people do not engage, they will start pushing even harder. They know how to increase the pressure to motivate others to perform.

Growth Areas

They often lack patience. They are quick to increase the tension to move things forward, even if the stress is unhealthy for some of the team members. They exaggerate the importance of the immediate results. Most people do not live up to their expectations. They struggle with people who do not deliver and have difficulty listening and absorbing the other person's point of view. They may become defensive when someone is challenging their ideas. They may set up win/lose debates. They may judge leaders or others who are not keeping up to their pace. They have a hard time slowing down to really understand what others are communicating. They may have difficulty admitting they are wrong or apologizing.

They can struggle with people who are not competent. They understand how relationships work and, sometimes, will use that information to get what they want. They can be perceived as demanding and not seeing the value of everyone on the team.

Motivations

They are typically hard-working and diligent. They hit deadlines and often exceed expectations. The downside is, if they do not work on listening and bringing others along, they will reach a professional ceiling. People may see them as corporate climbers without the care and consideration of others. They will do well at leading the tasks but may have trouble creating a shared vision with the team.

They may struggle building strong relationships with people who feel pushed. In order to ensure balanced relationships, Drivers are wise to ask for feedback and act on it. Instead of trusting their own instincts for every decision, they will need input from others. This healthy debate will drive additional individual and team success.

Interactions

Drivers will push. They struggle with others who are not achieving the results. They are great at coaching others; however, sometimes, it can come across as a win/lose conversation. Drivers will often need to revisit conversations and, at times, apologize. They will need to acknowledge they are pushing too fast and ramping up the urgency to an unhealthy level. When they are coachable and flexible, they will find solutions that work best for everyone. They know pushing everything as a top priority does not work. There must be clear priorities and team alignment.

Drivers know they may force compliance, but others will become resentful. In the future, others may boycott decisions because they do not feel included in the decision-making process. It is always best for the Driver to reflect on the balance between accountability and appreciation. They know they need allies to reach their individual and organizational potential.

Conflict and Change

Drivers love change. They are willing to change quickly without all of the facts and want to see things moving. They enjoy high energy and fast-moving conversations. If you are communicating with a driver, you can be direct, challenging, and aggressive. They are looking for new ways to win and will often welcome innovative ideas.

Conflict is best handled with facts and specific examples, so they can clearly see the situation. They enjoy debate and will demonstrate strong opinions and expect you to do the same. If you are challenging their competency, be prepared for a defensive response. If you are challenging their approach, they will often be open to the discussion. If you convince them of your approach, they will strongly support new initiatives.

They are clear about what they want and they expect you to be clear on what you want. They are quick to provide solutions and may struggle listening if they lose interest. Any change that introduces more policies and procedures and is perceived to slow them down may be negatively received. Getting the job done is more important than following the rules. They will take care of customers first, and everything else is secondary. Once they understand how it helps serve the customers and is a necessary part of the business, they will learn how to complete the processes quickly and move on to serving customers.

CHAPTER 13

Confidence Profile: Convincer

Victor is a convincer. He prides himself on getting the answers correct. He does not need input from others because he has already found the best solution. He knows he needs others to carry out his plan, but he is often disappointed. When he takes time to communicate his plan, he is often frustrated because people question the plan and slow down the process. What he has realized over the years is that his plans are correct, and people should just trust him and implement them.

He prefers taking advice from people with legitimate credibility. One of his favorite phrases is, "What does the research tell us?" He does not believe in group think and often questions how things are being handled. If rational logic is not used, he will question the decision and the outcome. Everyone must be able to defend their position. He is often focused on influencing and convincing others to do things his way. He wants the organization to be successful and will not rest until he believes things are on the right path.

Top Value

Convincers are motivated by moments of accomplishment.

Ideal Environment

The Ideal Environment for a Convincer is one with clear roles and high competence.

Strengths:

They have a crystal-clear picture of success. They are extremely driven by results and ensuring the organization has unprecedented success. They will feel their role is to convince others to follow. They are open to the criticism of their ideas, but only if provided by someone they view as credible. They respect those who have a high level of competence. They are a great follower when they are brought into the project with a clear and credible plan. They will hit deadlines and serve customers well. They will not accept "no" for an answer. They will continue driving toward a result. They will revisit an issue until the proper solution is achieved. They will work very hard and will spend time away from work thinking about how to solve complicated and difficult problems. They may be viewed as strong and assertive and will do whatever it takes to accomplish the mission.

The customer will be thrilled because they hit the deadlines and expected deliverables. They believe more discussion will simply slow down the process. They want to be trusted to do their jobs and expect others to do the same. If issues crop up, they will address them directly and expect that they will not happen again. They are direct and will ensure a great result.

Growth Areas:

They can struggle forming strong relationships that do not feel transactional. They struggle with phrases like "We can't do that." Other people around them may feel unimportant like pawns in their game. It may appear that they are more interested in their own agenda than the agenda of others. They may assume others should have the same ambition and will have low empathy when that is not the case. It is difficult for them to admit when they are wrong or apologize. They may win battles but could be losing the war. They may achieve the results but do not bring others along, so the success may appear self-serving.

They may not notice the relational disconnects and will continue to push, even when they have lost support for the idea. They may believe they have the best solution in the room and no input is needed. They may view brainstorming or collaboration as a waste of time. They may not understand the value of a shared vision for a project. They struggle with the idea of compromise if it weakens the decision. It is hard for them to remember to check in on the status of relationships as much as status of the results. They will win most arguments and may not understand the negative relational impact of that dynamic.

They may not understand the value of relationships. Leaders who believe strong relationships are the foundation of a team will have a major disconnect with Convincers. Ironically, it is very difficult to convince Convincers. They believe they have the correct answers and it is their job to convince others of their plan. They will be open to new ideas if they are backed by facts and credibility, but it is difficult for them to fake interest. A Convincer's patience level for perceived incompetence is extremely low. The lack of patience can be triggered by one incorrect fact or mistake. Once the Convincer writes someone off, that person may be viewed as a barrier to getting the work done.

Motivations

The challenge is that when other people feel like they have no influence over the Convincer, they will give up. It will not be worth their effort; it is a waste of time. No one lives up to the Convincer's expectations. The message or perception is that the Convincer knows how to do every job better than the person doing it.

When the motivations of the Convincer are understood as wanting to help, they will share exciting and global visions. Convincers can provide a compelling plan and solutions to get there. They need to work on having regular feedback sessions to ensure others are aligned. These discussions can be contagious, as people are attracted to the urgency and momentum. They will produce extraordinary results quickly if they master the art of bringing others along.

Interactions

Convincers want the project to be successful. They understand the voice of the customer and will not allow excuses or a victim mentality to stall progress. They will call out limited thinking and areas that need to be addressed. They are not afraid of conflict and will address it, even if it is uncomfortable for others. When they introduce conflict, they do not address things personally; it is about the work. If someone's actions are placing the project at risk, those behaviors must be addressed.

They are not as comfortable with receiving feedback as they are at giving feedback. They need to work on understanding the emotions of conflict. Convincers need to be aware of the emotional health of the team. If the team feels that they are being pushed too hard for too long, burnout is a common outcome.

Convincers tend to dismiss the feedback of others if the person giving the feedback is not clear. They may choose perfection instead of excellence and progress. They may prefer being right over building strong relationships.

Conflict and Change

Convincers need to be convinced. Introducing change for the sake of change will not work. You will need to provide evidence to persuade them. It is best to include references to individuals they respect.

They know they need to work on relationships, so helping them see their blind spots in this area is a great strategy. They want to be included in the beginning of change initiatives. If they are not brought into the change and are not aligned with the solution, they will challenge the direction. They will return to the conflict as many times as needed in order to make the right decision. To Convincers, there is a right and wrong decision and if the right decision is not reached, they may comply, but they are frustrated and not surprised when the failure happens.

When you provide feedback to a Convincer, make sure it is an area where you add value. They assess and evaluate advice with scrutiny. They have strong instincts and they are usually right. If you are contradicting their approach, you will need to be prepared. Once they agree with the solution, they will be incredibly loyal and will influence others toward the change. They will advocate for customers and ensure the project succeeds.

Confidence Profile Summary

Most often, you will see confidence profiles sticking together with the profiles nearest their score. For example, it is common to see Peace Keepers with Friend Makers. They will get along great and will support each other. One of the challenges with Peace Keepers and Friend Makers is they can be slow moving, they can suffer from group think, and if you do not fit in their group, you may feel like an outsider unable to break in.

The Inquisitors and Negotiators often have great chemistry. They love discussing what if scenarios, but may not be quick to action. They like to philosophize and have healthy debates. To them, the quality and liveliness of the conversation is as important as the result. They love to dream and think about the future and new ideas, but when it comes to doing something with that conversation, they may be a bit slow to act.

Finally, the Ignitors and Convincers will work very well with each other. They will respect each other's opinions and will have a high degree of trust for each other because the perceived competence level will be very high. The danger with these connections is it can feel exclusive in that others do not measure up. They also may move too fast and leave a trail of broken relationships behind them.

Peace Keepers and Convincers will have the most challenging relationship. Peace Keepers want steadiness and a calm and planned work environment. Convincers want to keep moving and looking for the next big thing. The pace of change will be the most difficult area to find alignment. The key for these two profiles working together is to agree on the common purpose. Once reminded and anchored to the mission of the organization and understanding why the change needs to take place, both are more open to each other. This mutual understanding is critical and must be revisited when conflicts are not resolving.

Next are Friend Makers and Drivers. Drivers are willing to risk relationships to ensure the results are achieved. Friend Makers are willing to risk results to ensure the relationships are maintained. This fundamental difference is critical to understanding the other profile's perspective. In order to achieve success together, both sides must make a conscious effort to value the other perspective. Drivers must learn to increase the value of relationships and listen with the intent to understand. Asking two or three follow-up questions to Friend Makers is a great strategy to ensure the communication is based on shared meaning. Friend Makers must learn to advocate for themselves and create a clear picture of what they want. This will allow common ground for discussion. Friend Makers must also understand the risks of moving too slow. Drivers believe that organizations are either growing or dying. Friend Makers must increase their understanding that growth is necessary. Once they agree on the need to grow, they can debate the best form of growth and the pace needed to make it happen.

Inquisitors are the translators for Peace Keepers and Friend Makers. They understand the importance of taking time to develop a great plan that everyone is invested in implementing. They also understand the urgency to get things done. They can create alignment and provide a great perspective and insight to all of the Confidence Profiles. If they are not clear on the role of questions to unify, they can use questions to divide. They must understand their role is to seek clarification that leads to unification. They will often uncover the core issues that need to be addressed before progress can be achieved.

Negotiators clearly understand the need for urgency, excitement, and increased energy in the organization. They understand that Drivers and Convincers need to provide solutions quickly to customers. The goal for Negotiators is to understand that if they create an environment of flexibility and finding the best solution, the plan will be extremely strong. They ensure that all the profiles feel valued and heard. This inclusive approach will be unstoppable if everyone understands their role and the power of collective momentum. When everyone feels heard, the best solutions are discovered and executed. If Negotiators lean too heavily toward pleasing Drivers and Convincers, the other profiles will feel as though they were manipulated. Negotiators must remain as unbiased as possible and actively listen to all options. When Negotiators act as effective facilitators without a biased agenda, the best solutions are found. It is critical for Negotiators to value all input and rally all perspectives in the final decision-making process. This will ensure the results are achieved at the fastest pace possible while maintaining strong relationships.

The Confidence Profiles do not give us permission to label ourselves or others. Your profile is not an excuse to demonstrate over or under confidence. Your profile is simply your starting point. You deserve to love your work, and your Confidence Profile will help you understand your tendencies.

To discover your Confidence Profile, visit MyAuthenticConfidence.com and sign up for Authentic Confidence Online. This interactive course will explain the process and provide your Confidence Profile. Enter the code DREAM2020 and receive a discount. After you complete the Confidence Profile Assessment, you will receive a custom Confidence Profile Report, along with confidence building recommendations.

AUTHENTIC CONFIDENCE QUOTIENT (ACQ):

1 List your current Roles and Responsibilities. *(Your formal and informal areas of accountability)* **Examples:** *Vision, Strategy, Project Management, Coaching, Team Building, Healthy Conflict, Performance Management, Finance, Marketing, Sales, Presenting, Motivation, Communication*

1 ROLES/ RESPONSIBILITIES	**2** CURRENT CONFIDENCE	**3** LIMITING BELIEF	**4** FUTURE GOAL

2 Define the current level of confidence in each role. **(UC, AC or OC)**
   Under Confidence: Do I feel incompetent or unsure of myself in this area? **(UC)**
   Authentic Confidence: Do I have great relationships and results in this area? **(AC)**
   Over Confidence: Do I exaggerate my skills or accomplishments in this area? **(OC)**

3 What are the limiting beliefs I have in each role?
   (IE: "I lack experience, education, training"…)

4 Write one goal that will build Authentic Confidence.
   (IE: "I will deliver a successful presentation.")

   Communicating with Authentic Confidence:
      List your greatest strength: _____
      List one area of under confidence you would like to resolve: _____
      Statement of Authentic Confidence: _____

AUTHENTIC CONFIDENCE

CHAPTER 14

Authentic Confidence Quotient (ACQ)

Progress happens when we face our current confidence challenges and create a plan to resolve them.

I initially designed the **Authentic Confidence Quotient (ACQ)**, to understand my own confidence issues. The ACQ is a confidential assessment. You are the only one who will see this assessment, unless you decide to share it with others. This is critical in ensuring your assessment is honest.

This is a self-assessment because when dealing with confidence issues, it is critical for you to self-identify the issues. Being told you have confidence issues, is often not an effective strategy. For example, telling a coworker he is arrogant, will rarely lead to a productive conversation. However, if that coworker shares his struggle with over confidence, it often leads to a great discussion. Once the issue is self-identified, you will be invested in the process to resolve the issue.

The ACQ will walk you through how to identify your confidence issues. Then you will define one area to work on. Once you have decided on the confidence issue you want to resolve, the Career Confidence Guide covered in Phase III, will help you resolve this confidence issue. It is a cyclical process that will help you work through all of the confidence issues in your career.

Most organizations are afraid of the leadership flavor of the month. Consulting companies promise results, but when the project is done, you are left holding the bag on yet another failed engagement strategy. Employees are tired of being assessed and interviewed with little or nothing to show for it.

"How will this be any different?" is the question often asked. When I was the director of Organizational Development at a multinational business, I asked the same question.

Most of the leadership development strategies were either dated or unproven. I decided to research real stories of real leaders who actually lived it, not theories or philosophies but people in the trenches making leadership happen. Out of these real-life examples, Authentic Confidence was born. Many real-life stories have proven that this process is practical and effective.

To help you understand the Authentic Confidence Quotient (ACQ), I want to provide one of these stories. The following is a true story; however, the names have been changed to maintain confidentiality.

Lauren had just been passed over for a promotion. Prior to this moment, her career had been on a steady incline. She worked hard, kept her head down, and thought the results would take care of themselves. This time, that strategy did not work, and she was angry. Her boss, Jalen, had chosen a coworker named Charlie for the promotion, and Lauren was shocked.

"Hi, Lauren, have a seat. I want to talk to you about the senior director position you applied for," said her boss.

"Oh, great," she said. She was excited to hear the news. She had been working hard for years and believed she deserved this promotion.

"Listen, I want to get right to the point. We couldn't be happier with your performance, but we're planning to give Charlie the promotion. He's really stepped up to the plate, and we think he's earned it. I just want to give you a heads up before the announcement is made."

Shocked, she responded, "What! Jalen, you can't give it to him! He's not ready. This is ridiculous; I can't believe you're doing this to me."

"Hold on, Lauren. You're a great asset to this company and a great team player, but it's Charlie who's impressed the executive team. He—"

With tears in her eyes she interrupted him, "It's not fair. I worked so hard for this. It's not fair. If he gets the job, I will not work for him. Did you even fight for me?"

"Lauren," Jalen said, slightly annoyed. "Let me give you a piece of advice. You can blame me for this, or you can stop leading from the shadows. You have to start putting yourself out there; let everyone know what you bring to the table."

"Great, so now you're using my humility against me. Perfect." She turned and slammed the door on her way out.

In her mind, she had outworked Charlie in every project. Lauren had been coaching Charlie for years. Charlie used her as a sounding board for every project. She liked Charlie but couldn't believe that others couldn't see the difference in their skill levels. She did not handle the news well, and her boss, Jalen, was concerned about losing her, so he asked me to meet with her.

I'd been consulting for Lauren's organization on a variety of leadership topics for a few years. Lauren had an impressive resume, including an Ivy League college education, great people skills, and a strong work ethic. However, she'd been in the same role for the past several years and wanted more responsibility. She believed if she continued to work hard, kept her head down, and minded her own business, things would work out. However, a week after meeting with Jalen, she was still demoralized.

"Hi, Lauren," I began, "thanks for taking the time to meet with me. I heard the news about the senior director position, and Jalen told me some of the back story, but I'd like to get your perspective on things."

"Hey, Ben, I don't know what to say. I guess I'm frustrated and angry. Maybe Jalen is right. Maybe I'm not ready for this position. Maybe I don't have what it takes. I feel so defeated. I don't know where to go from here. I lost it in Jalen's office and, really, it had nothing to do with Charlie. You know, I like Charlie. It's not that I don't want him to be successful. It's just that I think he received the promotion at my expense. Honestly, no one knows how much of his success resulted from my efforts."

"Lauren, it's normal to feel what you're feeling. You believed you deserved the promotion and it was ripped away. You worked hard and helped Charlie, then when it's time to get your reward, it's given to him. What are you most frustrated about?" I asked.

"I'm most frustrated with myself," she said. "I should have known better. I knew the board and other key leaders would be involved in this decision, and I didn't take any time to build relationships with them or discuss my work."

"You aren't alone in this struggle," I remarked. "Maybe it's time to look at what happened and where you would like to go from here. If there are things getting in your way, we want to understand them and resolve them. I would like to talk to you about a self-assessment I use called the Authentic Confidence Quotient (ACQ)."

Immediately defensive, she responded, "Oh, come on, Ben! I've done a million of these assessments. I don't think that's the answer."

"Lauren, I get it. But this is different. This is a self-assessment that will help you clarify what's limiting your career."

"Well, tell me about it," she replied, forcing a smile.

"Let me give you a quick overview. I designed the ACQ to guide leaders through the process of identifying confidence issues, understanding why they exist, and creating a game plan to resolve them. Learning to be honest about both strengths and growth areas is essential to your path forward."

"Okay, but Ben, I don't really think the main problem is my confidence," she said.

"That's because you're thinking about confidence from a narrow perspective. All leaders have confidence issues. Every leader is either finding confidence or learning how to teach confidence to others. I'm also on my own confidence journey. I go through this same process quarterly to determine where I'm doing well and where I need work. There's no judgment here; we're all in the process of learning how to communicate with confidence. Is it possible that your confidence challenges stopped you from advocating for yourself?"

"Maybe," she agreed.

"Okay," I replied. "Let me explain the ACQ, and then you can decide if you would like to continue with the coaching process."

I explained the overview and why confidence issues are at the core of most career setbacks. She was then willing to listen, and we progressed through the self-evaluation. I explained the ACQ was confidential and we discuss together what to share with her boss. She understood the process and wanted to continue.

"There are four sections of the ACQ," I continued. "Each is intended to uncover confidence issues and provide the framework to do something about them. I'll serve as your guide to work through the results. So, what do you say? Are you ready to give it a go?"

Lauren responded, surprised, "Right now?"

"Sure. I've got this room reserved for the morning. It doesn't take long, and we'll work through the process together."

When we finished completing the ACQ, Lauren was smiling. "So, what did you think?" I asked.

She responded, "Well, prior to doing this, I would have told you my life wasn't going to change until my boss changed. Now I realize there are some things I need to work on."

As we chatted, it was obvious that her emotions were still raw. When it came to influencing her boss, she was under confident. She was frustrated with that relationship, and it plagued her. She did not know how to keep her boss and other influencers up to date about the great projects she was working on without bragging. She now realized that staying under the radar was no longer working. She needed to learn how to communicate her accomplishments.

She had a limiting belief that until her boss changed the way he operated, she would not be able to thrive. Lauren was waiting for Jalen to become a better leader before she could move forward. This was not working, and she was giving up control of her career to Jalen.

After some reflection, she realized the future goal for her career. She would focus on adding value to Jalen and everyone else in her organization. This allowed her to take control of her own career, and even if this promotion did not work out, she would be ready for the next one.

Lauren started communicating her value to others and it was noticed. Leaders started to request her input on projects, and she was approached for promotions outside of her department. She supported Jalen and the promotion of Charlie and took ownership of her own career development. She learned the power of communicating with Authentic Confidence. She was leading strong without bragging.

Lauren's response to the ACQ is a common one. Taking the assessment changed her self-awareness and gave her a great starting point to get her career back on track.

CHAPTER 15

Identify Your Confidence Challenges

S elf-awareness starts with taking an objective view of honest feedback and using it to move from obscurity to influence.

In 1969, an engineering student from MIT wanted to form a band and make a record. He invested his money to build a recording studio in his basement, and went to work. He found a friend to sing and he handled all the instrumentation. After two years, they submitted their demo to record companies, hoping to hit it big, but were turned down. Instead of being discouraged, they asked, "What can we do to improve?"

They listened to the feedback, worked hard, and submitted another demo again in 1973. Again, they were turned down, but not deterred. Once again, they asked, "What should we do to improve?" They continued to tour with the band they had formed and worked tirelessly to create a unique sound, something they could say was their own.

Finally, in 1976, with their backs against the wall, they submitted their music to the record companies one last time, all the while continuing to collect feedback and work on improving their sound.

This time, the response was different. The record companies were thrilled. They loved what they heard and wanted to sign them to a recording contract. They went from being rejected by everyone to everyone fighting over them. Many said it was the best music they had heard in years. This was a band that had been used to rejection and yet, they were resilient enough to keep taking the feedback and making the adjustments needed to improve.

The album they produced ended up becoming the most successful debut album at that time and it sold over 17 million copies. So, who were they? Well, they were just another band from the East Coast. They called themselves Boston. Boston's 1976 album, simply called *Boston*, was used as a benchmark for many aspiring artists. Most of that album still receives radio play today, more than 40 years after it was released. Boston learned to take feedback and translate it into action; as a result, they achieved amazing levels of success.

The ACQ will guide you through your self-awareness discovery process. You will be taking an honest look at what is working and what needs work. The following is an explanation of the four sections of the ACQ.

The four sections of the ACQ include:
1. **List your current Roles and Responsibilities.**
2. **Define the current level of confidence in each role.**
3. **What are the limiting beliefs you have in each role.**

4. **Write a future goal that will build Authentic Confidence.**

Finally, you will **list your greatest strength**, **one area of under confidence to resolve,** and then, create your **Statement of Authentic Confidence**.

Section 1. Roles and Responsibilities

In the first section, you will identify the roles and responsibilities you face in your current position. The purpose of this section is to identify all the major areas of responsibility in your role. This is not your title; it is what you do, including your priorities each day.

Lauren's roles included Leading Up (influencing her boss), Leading Around (influencing her peers), Leading With (influencing her direct reports), Communication (verbal and written), Conflict Resolution, Customer Service, Training Presentations, Area Strategic Planning, and Budget Management. The responsibilities listed should be those that determine your level of success. Once all roles and responsibilities are written down, it is time to evaluate how you are doing in each area.

Section 2. Current Confidence

Next, define your current level of confidence in each role. Determine whether you have under confidence (UC), Authentic Confidence (AC), or over confidence (OC) in each area. If you are unsure of yourself, you would list that area as under confidence or UC. If you had great results and relationships in that area, you would list that as Authentic Confidence or AC. If you find yourself exaggerating in an area, you would list that role as over confident or OC.

Keep in mind, there are no right or wrong answers. The goal is an honest evaluation. Believing you are an insecure person because you have some areas of under confidence is not helpful. That is a label and a judgment. It is also not helpful to believe you are a better human being than others. It is helpful to understand that you, like most people, are on a confidence journey. If you don't have any areas of under confidence, you are not being stretched.

Once you have identified problem areas, you can then create a plan to overcome your confidence issues in those areas. This will allow you to define the problem and create a plan to move forward. You cannot solve problems you do not define.

Section 3. Limiting Belief

The third section looks at limiting beliefs. Limiting beliefs are the thoughts you have about your career that hold you back. Negative self-talk creates fear, doubt, or anxiety about an aspect of your career. If left unchecked, limiting beliefs can spread into other areas of your life and create frustration. This can leave you feeling stuck with no options.

Lauren's limiting belief was "My relationship with my boss is never going to change." This notion created an insurmountable barrier to progress. It shut down communication and killed hope. As a result, she felt stuck in blame and saw no way out.

Typically, there aren't limiting beliefs in areas of Authentic Confidence. However, at the core of every over or under confident area is a limiting belief.

The way to determine a limiting belief is to think about why you feel unsure of yourself in this area. Think back to the first negative experience and think about the memory that bothered you. Some examples include:

I am not smart enough,

I do not have the experience,

I do not have the training,

No one values me in this area,

I always fail,

No one cares, and

My boss will never understand me.

These are dangerous beliefs, that can hold you back. The goal is to conquer these limiting beliefs by understanding them and creating a plan to replace them.

Section 4. Future Goal

The final section is determining your future goal. This is where the work begins. Up to this point, you have been working on defining the problem. Now it is time to define the solution. What does success look like in every area of over or under confidence? It does not work to simply eliminate the limiting belief; you must find a replacement belief. When you describe how you want your career to work in that area, you will make steps to make that preferred future a reality. Visualize a future goal as clearly as you can. This will create an image that will inspire action.

I want to make one point clear. It has been proven that self-affirmations connected to unrealistic goals do not work. For example, I love basketball and I'd love to play in the National Basketball Association (NBA). I can look in the mirror every day and say, "I am going to play professionally in the NBA," but, trust me, it will not happen. I am a slow 5'9" Norwegian American who cannot jump. Last time I checked, that will not get me in the NBA. Self-affirmations are not going to change that.

However, self-affirmations connected to realistic goals absolutely work.

Lauren gained control over her goals. Over time, she was able to think differently about her boss and find ways to add value. She learned how to become a major influencer and use her problem-solving skills to find new ways to communicate with others. She took ownership of her accomplishments and accepted the encouragement and compliments of others. This self-affirmation allowed her to enter situations with a new presence and positive energy. It was attractive and contagious. People wanted her in the room to contribute.

List Your Greatest Strength

The next question in the assessment asks you to list your greatest strength. One of the keys to communicating with Authentic Confidence is learning how to be comfortable describing your strengths. Some people believe if they own a strength it is viewed as arrogance. This can be true, but not if you handle it authentically.

When you walk into a store to purchase a service, you want the person providing that service to believe they are good at what they do. If you are having new appliances installed in your house, you want the installers to know what they are doing. This is not arrogance; it is competence. If they are unable to communicate their competence in clear terms, you will lose confidence in them.

I recommend starting out by becoming comfortable with a specific strength. For Lauren, it was solving problems. She learned to be comfortable raising her hand to help anytime someone was stuck with a difficult problem. She eventually learned how to communicate this strength in a way that was comfortable for her, until she could eventually say, "I love working with people and solving challenging problems."

She learned to share success stories that demonstrated her competence. She was not bragging about herself; she was providing factual stories about how she helped others.

Others assumed that Lauren was competent in this area and willing to lend her expertise as needed. She did not claim she was great at everything or that being a great problem solver made her a better person than others; she simply stood her ground in this area and was no longer afraid to speak up about her ability to positively impact a situation.

Area of Under Confidence

The second statement asks you to look at your areas of under confidence and select one. Think about the area that would allow you to move forward in your career if you resolved it. For example, with Lauren, it was Leading Up. She wanted to develop a better strategy to communicate with her boss. She wanted to be able to speak up and feel comfortable sharing her ideas. For you, it might be public speaking, dealing with conflict, selling, performance evaluations, or team development. Whatever it is, make sure it will have an impact.

Lauren needed to learn how to work with her boss if she wanted to avoid hitting the ceiling in her career. This is the area Lauren and I worked on, and it paid off.

Select an area that is significant in your role and one in which you can make meaningful progress in the next three to six months. Now that you have selected the area of under confidence that you are going to work on, you will define success. We'll be working on creating a plan to resolve this under confidence issue in the remaining chapters of this book.

Statement of Authentic Confidence

The final area is your Statement of Authentic Confidence. This is one area that you can share with others. Here, you will combine your greatest strength and area of under confidence in one statement. For example, Lauren's Statement of Authentic Confidence was, "I love helping people solve problems and I'm working on better communication." This is a statement where she is learning how to become equally comfortable with a strength and growth area. When she shared this with her team, it allowed others around her to do the same. No one was expecting perfection any longer; it was about focusing on progress.

One of my favorite examples is Mike Krzyzewski (Coach K), the head coach of Duke's basketball team. He says that West Point gave him the opportunity to be proud every day of his life and, likewise, he creates an environment where people can be great at Duke. He was not the greatest player of all time, and he is the first one to admit he had many things to work on when it came to his game.

He shared an example of when he coached the Olympic basketball team.

Coach K was in the gym after practice when Michael Jordan walked in. Jordan started shooting around and asked the coach to come over to give him any advice.

Coach K was amazed that the greatest basketball player of all time was asking for his advice. Michael was a great player, and he wanted to become a better shooter. He was equally comfortable with his greatness and growth areas and was willing to work on improving.

I think we all work in that type of environment. We want to work for a great coach, yet we are often hesitant to become one. We want someone who inspires us and believes in our capabilities. That is what others also want from us.

The purpose of the Statement of Authentic Confidence is to first believe your greatness internally. Once you believe it internally, you will find ways to demonstrate it externally. Once you own our greatness, sharing a growth area will demonstrate your humility. Your statement of Authentic Confidence may be: "I enjoy coaching others and I am working on my conflict resolution skills." In every important area of your life, you should believe you are on the path to becoming great.

For example, before I speak in front of a group, my statement of Authentic Confidence is "I love teaching and I am working on connecting with every person." This is valuable to me, especially if I am feeling under confident. Something happens when I remind myself that I love to teach and I am still growing in my ability to connect. It sets the tone for the event and creates an energy that instantly puts me in the right frame of mind. It is a self-affirmation tied to a realistic plan. It is a mindset shift that creates a path toward Authentic Confidence. If you want to become a great leader, the first step is to believe it is possible.

Results

Now that you have completed the assessment, let's review the results. If you have under confidence in every area of your career, do not panic. You are now on the journey to do something about it. You may be in a new role, or you may be struggling to find your place. In Phase III, we will walk you through the step-by-step process to find competence and confidence in your role.

If you have Authentic Confidence in every area of your career, there are most likely two options: Either you have dominated your current role and you are ready for a new one, or you have low self-awareness.

If you have great results and relationships in every area of your current role, and others would agree, then you are ready for the next challenge. The most common next step would be to talk to your boss about new opportunities.

The more common reason for listing Authentic Confidence for every area is connected to low self-awareness. For example, I had a client who believed he had Authentic Confidence in every area of his career. When we met, I asked him what he was working on. He said he was not working on anything. He believed he was not the issue; it was everyone around him. I simply asked him to own his role in the relationships around him not working. Eventually, he admitted that he was under confident in some areas and over confident in others. Although the process was uncomfortable for him, he took it to heart and his influence grew significantly. Even the greatest leaders in the world are working on continual improvement.

The most common results of the ACQ are a combination of over, under, and Authentic Confidence. You may be doing well in some areas while other areas need work. This is normal, and no matter how long you have been in your role, there is no judgment. The goal is to help you clarify where you are doing well and what needs some additional attention.

Now, it is time to select one area of under confidence that you want to resolve. It should be an area that will lead to significant progress in your role.

For a FREE download of the Authentic Confidence Quotient, visit ConfidenceKit.BenFauske.com.

Discover the Pattern of World-Class Influencers

CHAPTER 16

The 5 Stages of Career Confidence
(Career Confidence Guide)

t is now time to reveal the pattern that changed my career. As I was researching recording artists, I noticed they all followed the same steps to move from obscurity to influence.

I discovered The 5 Stages of Career Confidence when I was learning about the Beatles and Elvis. Elvis Presley grew up in humble circumstances. He was a bit of an outsider and his family struggled to make ends meet. Elvis wanted desperately to ease their financial burden. He would tell his mom over and over that someday, he would buy her a Cadillac. Someday, he would buy her a house with a garden and she wouldn't have to worry any more. He promised to take care of her. Elvis was determined to do something meaningful with his life and realized music was his best chance. He wanted a career of **Significance**.

When Elvis and his family moved to Memphis, Tennessee, as a young boy, he quickly discovered a place called Beale Street. He was mesmerized by the blues music he experienced there. He wanted to make music, but not just any music; he wanted to make the kind of music that would make people feel something like he did on Beale Street. He would listen to artists like Arthur Crudup, B.B. King, and Muddy Waters, and it transformed him from a shy young man into a confident performer. He grew his **Competence** by imitating the masters.

Every day for months and months, he stopped by the local music store and asked if he could make a record. The answer was the same over and over again, "No." The record company did not believe he had anything special, but he did not give up. He kept coming, day after day.

Eventually, he wore them out and they recorded his music because he wouldn't take no for an answer. He was going to make his career happen and no one was going to stop him. He had learned from his heroes that eventually you have to create your own sound. It was time for him to demonstrate his **Authenticity**.

When Elvis released his recording, he broke through barriers. He appealed to a wide audience based on his unique sound. He learned quickly that he was in demand and would be touring around the world promoting his music and providing a better life for his parents. Once he understood his value, he learned how to **Leverage** his efforts. He was no longer a shy boy waiting to be invited in. He was an assertive performer, looking to positively influence others with his music.

Finally, he never forgot his roots. When anyone would ask for his help, he was there. He was beyond generous to others. He wanted nothing more than to make friends and serve. He served his country without complaint; he entertained his fans like no one had ever done before, and he was devoted to his family. He was not perfect, and made many mistakes, but he definitely demonstrated **Empathy** toward others.

All the artists I studied were inspired and had a desire to do something with their lives. They each had moments of impact when they realized they wanted to do something significant.

Something stuck with me about that story. Elvis did not just wake up one day deciding to be great, and it happened. He spent years studying his heroes. He perfected their sound, and then he created his own style, which he shared with the world. The rest is history.

His story piqued my curiosity, so I took on the quest to find out why musicians were successful. My research included the following artists: The Beatles (Paul McCartney), Beach Boys (Brian Wilson), Fleetwood Mac (Mic Fleetwood), Billy Joel, Elton John, Blonde (Debbie Harry), Adele, Taylor Swift, Bob Dylan, Woody Guthrie, The Rolling Stones (Keith Richards), Run DMC (Darryl McDaniels), Eminem, Garth Brooks, George Strait, Phil Collins, Heart (Ann and Nancy Wilson), The Who (Pete Townshend), Metallica, Def Leppard, Jimi Hendrix, Beastie Boys, Sara Bareilles, Journey (Steve Perry and Jonathan Cain), Chicago, Elvis Costello, Joni Mitchell, Don Williams,

MercyMe, Steven Curtis Chapman, Rich Mullins, Keith Green, Tom Petty, Daryl Hall and John Oates, John Mayer, Jason Mraz, Kem, Kenny Rogers, Carly Simon, Willie Nelson, Amy Grant, Leonard Cohen, Crosby, Stills and Nash (Graham Nash), Rod Stewart, The Smiths, Morrissey, Johnny Marr, Bob Marley, Charlie Daniels, Randy Travis, Everything But the Girl (Tracey Thorn), Carole King, Neil Young, Johnny Cash, Frank Sinatra, James Taylor, Simon and Garfunkel, Prince, Michael Jackson, Tina Marie, Rick James, James Brown, Barry White, Michael W. Smith, Newsboys, Anne Murray, Pavarotti, Simply Red, U2, and Madonna. There were countless others along with hours of interviews, trips to the Rock and Roll Hall of Fame, and video footage.

What do all of these artists have in common? The more I studied them, the more I realized they took the same journey to success. They started in the same place and reached the pinnacles of their careers in the same manner.

The secret pattern is captured in the Career Confidence Guide and covers The 5 Stages of Career Confidence. This is a skills development process designed to help you build an unstoppable career. We'll use the Career Confidence Guide to help you resolve your confidence challenges.

I applied it to my life, and, over the years, I have coached thousands of others on the process. It applies not only to music but also to business, sports, government agencies, and nonprofits. All have applied this pattern to find unprecedented levels of success. The rest of the book will explain these 5 stages in detail, and teach you how to apply them to your life at work.

In my research, I wanted to start with the best: The artists who dominated every decade, starting in the 1950s. Who had significant influence in the early days of rock and roll? It was the boy who grew up in Memphis, Tennessee, and was influenced by the delta blues. He grew up in an era when rhythm and blues artists were not played on the airwaves, yet young Elvis Presley was hypnotized by the power of this music. He took the world by storm and became the King of Rock and Roll.

In the 1960s, there were four boys from Liverpool who called themselves the Beatles. Many believe the Beatles were the greatest band of all time and that no one will ever match their accomplishments.

Then in the 1970s, came a unique sound that many deemed as a shallow fad, but most agree this band perfected the sound. They were brothers first known as The Brothers Gibb and eventually changed their name to The Bee Gees.

In the 1980s came the child star turned King of Pop. His album, *Thriller,* became one of the largest selling albums of all time. In his later life, he was a controversial figure, but no one can argue about the influence Michael Jackson had on popular music.

The 1990s was the first time a non-pop-music artist would be a dominant artist. He came on the scene with a larger-than-life personality, jumping off amplifiers and running around the stage for his unprecedented live performances. With the influence of George Strait, Garth Brooks became an enigmatic performer in the 90s. He sold out arenas all around the country and, after taking 10 years off from the music business, came back on the scene and continued right where he left off.

In the 2000s, the same phenomenon happened with another non-pop-music artist. This hard-working kid from Detroit would redefine the genre and handle issues rarely—if ever—approached by an artist before. His birth name was Marshal Mathers, and he goes by the stage name Eminem.

In the 2010s, Taylor Swift was—and still is today—smashing the charts. When she listened to Shania Twain, it made her want to run around the block and dream about what she could accomplish. Shania revealed a world where Taylor could channel all of her frustrations. She had been teased and felt like a misfit for much of her childhood, and music was her escape. She loved it. Taylor Swift has redefined herself many times and has designed her own version of what makes a successful female recording artist.

All of the artists I studied followed a similar journey. I looked at some of the greatest musical artists from every decade starting with the 1950s and working through the 2010s. I chose a dominant artist from each decade and analyzed the pattern they followed to achieve success.

In the Career Building Phase III, you will find your hero, identify the gaps between you and your hero, and close those gaps. The Career Confidence Guide, based on The 5 Stages of Career Confidence, is the blueprint you will use to determine your career plan.

CAREER CONFIDENCE GUIDE

OBJECTIVE:

The Career Confidence Guide is for every employee to map out future career goals. It is intended to provide a clear picture of future success. Employees and managers brainstorm potential development options and create an action plan. This leads to a career development plan as well as an individual development plan. The Guide should be reviewed quarterly to ensure successful resolution.

Significance: What is the area of under confidence you want to resolve? _____
Define success in this area? What is the size and scope?

Competence: Who has the needed skill? What is your plan to learn the skill?
What are the next steps?

Authenticity: How will you know when you have mastered the skill?
How will you make it your own?

Leverage: How will this skill change your career? How will it change your life?
How will you celebrate and communicate your Authentic Confidence in this area?

Empathy: Who will hold you accountable and encourage your progress?
How will you use this skill to help others? How will this skill change their lives?
How will you teach this skill to others?

Next Actions: _____

CHAPTER 17

Significance
(Moment of Impact)

Career Significance is when you make the decision to have a meaningful impact with your work. Elvis was inspired by Muddy Waters. The Beatles were inspired by Elvis and Buddy Holly. John Lennon said that the first time he heard Buddy Holly; it was as though time stood still.

The Beatles were not alone; all the artists I read about loved their work. For the Beatles, it was personal. John Lennon and Paul McCartney had both lost their mothers as young boys and had a strong bond; they were determined to do something significant with their lives. They challenged each other to make great music, and they did.

The Bee Gees were a group of three brothers who loved music at an early age. Their early mentors were the Beatles, and they would stop at nothing to find their own place in music. Early in their career they were criticized for sounding like a Beatles cover band. But they evolved and went on to sell millions of records in their very own style of music, dominating the charts of the 1970s.

Michael Jackson was part of the group, The Jackson 5, in the middle of the Motown movement of Detroit city. When he saw artists dance, he would study them and learn how to be more than just a singer; he wanted to be an entertainer. Music was his passion and what he wanted to pursue. When Michael Jackson watched performances of James Brown, he was mesmerized. The way James Brown moved and sang on stage was contagious. People went crazy watching James Brown and Michael desperately wanted to have a similar impact on his fans.

The first time Garth Brooks heard George Strait on the radio, he decided to pursue music no matter what the cost. Garth Brooks said his world stood still when he heard George for the first time. Garth knew he wanted to make music, but he also wanted to make a difference with the music he wrote. He wanted to be one of the greatest, and George Strait was a major influence along with his dad's heroes, George Jones and Merle Haggard. These men would be the background to his success.

Similarly, Eminem grew up battling other rap artists in the making. He knew it was the best way to break out of his difficult situation. Eminem was from 8 Mile Road in Detroit, a tough neighborhood, and he struggled with a tough family situation. He grew up listening to Run-DMC and LL Cool J, among others. Rap music was his way out. He believed it was his best option to provide his family with the life that he never had. It motivated him to work harder and continue to reinvent himself so that he could stay relevant in a world that was not always welcoming to him. He wanted to make his mark on the music industry, and he did just that.

No woman in the history of popular music has broken onto the scene like Taylor Swift. Very few artists have had the ability to break through at such a young age and find sustained success. She demonstrated poise and resilience when the chronically over confident Kanye West disrupted her acceptance speech at the Video Music Awards (VMAs). Taylor won the award for best female music video in 2009, and Kanye walked on stage, took her microphone, and told the crowd that Beyoncé had one of the best videos of all time. Taylor was visibly shaken, but proceeded to handle the situation with class. She showed the world her authentic self and that has translated to a powerful connection. In the process, she shattered nearly every sales record and continues to win awards from her peers and fans.

Another artist who has dominated the airwaves in recent years is Adele. After hearing Etta James sing, she said, "She was the first time a voice made me stop what I was doing and sit down and listen. It took over my mind and body." Adele is courageous and determined to let the world know she is comfortable and confident with herself. Her first three albums have dominated the airwaves and she is just getting started. Her work is universally admired and wins new audiences every day. This desire to make a difference is the first step in your career design.

Significance is found through continued growth. By gaining new leadership skills and resolving your confidence issues, your influence will increase, and so will the opportunities that cross your path.

When you completed the Authentic Confidence Quotient (ACQ), you selected one area of under confidence that you wanted to resolve in your career. What will it look like to overcome this issue? How will your life be different once you have conquered it?

It's important to visualize your highlight reel in this area; that means picturing or visualizing success. For decades, Olympians have been picturing victory in their minds before competitions. A clear and compelling picture of winning and overcoming obstacles has been proven to increase the odds of success.

So think in detail about the confidence issue on which you are working. Imagine different scenarios—including potential obstacles—and you will be drawn to solutions that make that image a reality. The biggest mistake most people make in their careers is not knowing where they are going. They do not have a clear definition of what success looks like. They are simply drifting through life, paying the bills, and surviving work until the weekend. That is a defeating pattern. Avoid it by defining what you want out of your career.

If the confidence issue you chose is public speaking, success might be presenting in front of your team without stress. If you chose leading up, it might be having a great conversation with your boss once per week. Whatever your goal is for significance, you should be able to resolve this issue in the next three to six months.

For example, one of my clients defined communication as his area of under confidence. Communication is a broad topic and consequently hard to nail down. So, instead, we decided to work on the specific skill of making presentations to his boss. He was not happy with the effectiveness of his public speaking skills and wanted them to be effective and engaging. He then defined success in this area as the ability to effectively present a new idea to his boss without stress. The size and scope of this idea was realistic.

When trying to determine the correct size and scope of a goal, choose something that is under your control and you can complete in three to six months. If the timeframe is longer, it is hard to stay focused, and you can lose hope. If it is shorter, the goal probably is not significant. The power of this timeframe is that, once you find Authentic Confidence in one area, you can move on to the next and potentially resolve two to four confidence issues per year.

CHAPTER 18

Competence
(Model the Master)

To grow your Competence, it is critical to find someone who has been where you would like to go. The Beatles did just that. Growing up in Liverpool, the Beatles had modest beginnings. They struggled to find success as a band. They entered every talent contest they could find in the early days and lost every time. There were hundreds of other bands covering the same music and they couldn't find a way to break through, so they decided to study Buddy Holly.

They learned his hits and also the B-side songs and obscure records. They perfected them all. This allowed them to play for hours and other bands couldn't keep up. They understood the structure of Buddy Holly's songs and realized they could emulate his formula for success. They modeled their early career after him, even down to John Lennon wearing glasses.

Prior to this point, John Lennon would walk around bumping into things, as it was not cool to wear glasses. After Buddy Holly, John wore his glasses with pride and mimicked the confidence Buddy had in writing and recording songs with meaningful lyrics. At this point, the Beatles started to separate themselves from other bands and started to master their own version of Buddy's songs. This would become the foundation for their success.

For Elvis, it was Muddy Waters. When you listen to Elvis Presley's first hit record, it was a rhythm and blues song, "That's Alright". He mastered his version of the blues sound of Muddy Waters and Memphis. The same was true for the Beatles. Their breakthrough on the Ed Sullivan show was a tune called "I Want to Hold Your Hand." It could have come right off a Buddy Holly album.

When the Bee Gees released their first album, they sounded just like the Beatles. Their opening song, "Turn of the Century" was a clone of early Beatles' music. They started out emulating the Beatles—that was their foundation—and then they found their own sound.

Each of the artists listed below modeled their music after another artist who inspired them.

The principle is the same in leadership. If you select a desired leadership competence and emulate a leader with that skill, you will be on the path to finding new levels of excellence in your work.

I studied hundreds of recording artists. The following group was particularly interesting because they found the highest levels of influence in each decade. All of these artists were invested in their own development, the success of their band, and delivered at a high level for their fans. In order to take pride in their work, the artists needed a level of competence. None of them started out famous, and, contrary to popular belief, none of them were overnight successes. They all started out by emulating their heroes. They all started out learning from artists who had gone before them and paved the way for their success. The following are the artists that I studied:

Decade	Artist of the Decade	Influence
1950s	Elvis Presley	Muddy Waters
1960s	The Beatles	Buddy Holly
1970s	The Bee Gees	The Beatles
1980s	Michael Jackson	James Brown
1990s	Garth Brooks	George Strait
2000s	Eminem	Run DMC
2010s	Taylor Swift	Shania Twain

Why did they all copy other artists? Why didn't they start out with their own sound?

This is the mistake many of us make in our careers. We decide on a path and blaze our own trail in an attempt to create an amazing career on our own. We do not want to copy someone else; we want to make it on our own.

That was my problem. I had worked eight jobs in eight years, and they were all in different fields. Instead of gaining momentum in one area, I hopped around from one career to the next.

Every great leader I studied was first an apprentice. People often skip this step in developing their careers, except, for example, in the construction trades where everyone realizes the importance of mastering work skills before working alone. What if they did not have an apprenticeship program? What would happen if someone decided they wanted to be a homebuilder without the apprenticeship process? What if someone just woke up one day and decided to build a house? Imagine what that house would look like. Imagine how it would hold up. Having gone through the homebuilding process, there's no way I would trust someone who had no training or apprenticeship process to build my house.

Yet, when it comes to leadership, we do it all the time. The attitude is "Sure, I will take on this new role and make it happen. I will take on this new task and, even though I was never properly trained and never went through an apprenticeship from anyone, I will give it a shot." I see this most often with new supervisors. They were successful and fully trained at their previous position and excelled. They demonstrated some leadership abilities and so the organization moved them into supervision. All of the hours spent training and honing their skills at a technical level are a given; but to spend that same amount of time training them to lead would be seen as ridiculous. So, instead, they are thrust into the position and asked to sink or swim. Because they knew how to do the old job, they are expected to figure out the new job; some do and some do not. But even the ones that do are like homebuilders with no experience. They may produce results for a season, but if their leadership foundation is not strong, the walls will start caving in. Things look great on the outside, but they are simply covering up the chaos and instability inside.

It's a mistake to skip the apprenticeship process. It is important to find others who can help pave the way to success. Although new leaders want to skip this part, they would succeed faster by learning from experienced leaders who can teach the keys to success. They can teach the situations to avoid and, thereby, save years of frustration.

If you do not learn to master the competence of another expert, you will have to start from scratch. You can accomplish many things in your career, but if you go it on your own, it could take a lifetime of trial and error. You will be attempting to build a house with no experience and no blueprint. The lack of a model can leave you frustrated and often feeling stuck with your own development and that of your team.

Mastering the competence model provides a framework from which to start. It provides momentum and a game plan for early success. It minimizes unnecessary drama and increases your ability to focus on what really matters. *Competence* is defined as the ability to do something successfully or efficiently.

In order to grow your area of under confidence, you will first find a mentor. Look for someone you admire who will help you master this skill. There will be time for you to develop your own version and put your own unique imprint on this competence, but not in this step. In this step, you want to master the model, and you will quickly see an increase in your effectiveness. Your customers and teammates will see a marked improvement in what you deliver, and your boss will be thrilled with your increased productivity.

When working with a mentor, you want to learn as much as possible about why they do things a certain way. They will also serve as a sounding board and source of encouragement for the next steps in the process. Keep in mind; you do not need a mentoring program in your organization to start. You are not asking for a lifetime commitment; you just need to find someone willing to help you in this one specific area. That person might even work for another company. They just need to be great at the skill you wish to develop.

Another common pitfall for leaders in this phase is trying to learn from everyone. They are reading leadership books from Mother Teresa, General Patton, Oprah, and Jack Welch. The problem with this scattered approach is what I call leadership dabbling. You marginalize your skills and effectiveness every time you dilute your leadership style. You learn to dabble with a bunch of leadership styles and techniques, but you never perfect any of them. If you want to be a great leader and accelerate your level of competence, you have to master the leadership style of someone you admire. Learn, read, and absorb everything you can from one person. This is the most effective way to elevate your confidence in this area.

Each artist I mentioned above started by performing an identical cover of their hero. Then they produced a song that was one step removed from a cover. It was their own song, but it definitely emulated their heroes. Then they moved to their own songs and their own sound. None of the artists started with an original sound. They started by mimicking their idols in great detail. If you want to take pride in your work, this is the evolution of confidence. It does not happen by rolling out of bed and creating the greatest song ever. It is a process of learning about what makes great music.

In the same way, we cannot expect to roll out of bed and be great leaders. We must find a leadership mentor who has paved the way in our chosen field. We must learn everything we can about why they are successful and what they did to achieve success. We must take everything we can and put it into action. We must learn to lead as they led before us. Then, when we master the leadership skills they have demonstrated for us, we can branch out on our own and determine our own leadership style. Until we learn the competence of our mentors, we will likely have major leadership delays.

When starting out, the artists were very selective about whom to emulate. They chose only the artists who really moved them, inspired them, and whom they respected. They did not copy everyone. This allowed them to perfect the sound that they admired.

We must select someone who inspires us to lead well, inspires us to take the right actions, and is living the life we would like to lead. Then you can move to the next step in the process and start creating your own sound and style. It all starts with selecting the right mentor who has mastered the right competence.

One of my clients came up to me after a team session. She mentioned that she selected a global leadership mentor. She explained to me that since selecting this mentor, her life had not been the same. She listened to her mentor every day and instead of living by her mood swings, she was living by his clear and steady advice. She said her team had noticed a difference in her consistent enthusiasm and they appreciated her newfound steadiness. She shared that she planned to attend a conference by this individual, and on implementing his teachings with her team. The engagement level of the team continued to rise, and she shared with them what she learned every day and they then discussed application together as a team.

In order to find competence for yourself, you must start with your mentor in this area. Who has gone where you would like to go? It does not mean you have to find someone whom you want to emulate in every part of life but just someone you would like to emulate in this specific skill. Many of your mentors will be great in one area, but not great in other areas. Select someone who is gifted in the area in which you are under confident. After you select a mentor, you will need to create a plan to learn from them.

Learning from your mentor is as simple as setting up an informal meeting to learn the best practices of your desired skill. Most mentors will be flattered that you want to learn from them. I recommend reaching out to them and asking them for one hour of their time. You are not asking them to be your mentor the rest of your life. You are simply asking them to help you learn one specific skill and help you overcome your area of under confidence. Come prepared for the meeting with questions on how they deliver excellence in this area. Talk specifically about what they do and what they recommend for your situation. Take good notes and thank them for their time. Sometimes, you will need additional meetings; sometimes, you will gather everything you need in one meeting. This will be your blueprint to resolving this issue. It is a customized approach from someone you admire. This blueprint will provide the motivation to keep you moving toward your goal.

Some clients will say, "I don't know anyone who has the skill I need." They want to skip this step of the process and come back to it later. If you do not select a mentor, you will likely remain stuck in your area of under confidence. If you knew how to resolve your confidence issue in this area, you would have already done it. Selecting a mentor creates hope. When someone has overcome the issue you are facing, they have unique insights that are invaluable to your progress. Don't wait to complete the process until you find the perfect mentor. If the mentor you are selecting is not the perfect person, they will likely have some valuable insights and they may point you to a mentor who is a better fit. Start the journey with someone, as this progress will allow you to resolve the issue.

One client struggled with handling conflict. He selected a mentor who shared a simple technique for tough conversations. This approach was quick, easy, and served him well.

My client quickly adopted this strategy and he said his conflicts transitioned from uncomfortable to productive immediately. He was still uncomfortable with conflict, but this was a great strategy to start reducing the amount of stress he felt when dealing with difficult people. This small step before combative conversations helped him to remain calm.

CHAPTER 19

Authenticity
(Signature Creation)

We were designed for unique contribution and **anything less is to sacrifice our potential.** Authenticity is the discovery and display of our individual value to others. Adele has demonstrated authenticity in many ways. The majority of female recording artists were coerced to fit into a certain mold. Adele did not buy into these shallow expectations. She has been known to stop working with people who want her to change.

Adele knows who she is and who she is not. She has a style and persona all her own, and it works. She lives authentically. However, even Adele started out by studying and mastering the great artists she admired, like Etta James. Then, with that foundation, she created her own sound and carved her own path. Many people believe she was an overnight sensation. The truth is that she spent countless hours mastering the sound of other artists before her sound took over the music world. When she found her own voice, great things happened. Her second album became the biggest selling digital album of all time in the United States. British singer and songwriter Elton John stated, "She's authentic, she doesn't lip sync, she comes on and she sings, she's the real deal. She's not slick, she's human, she's imperfect, she's what every entertainer should be." This is what can happen in our careers when we move from imitation to creation.

Johnny Cash was a struggling musician, unable to provide for his young family. When he finally had the chance to perform for a record producer, he sang his heart out. The problem was that he sounded like everyone else. He was singing the same old worn out gospel songs that had been covered thousands of times. At that moment, Johnny realized the only chance he had to make an impact was to do something radical. He was at the end of his rope and felt he had nothing left to lose, so he went with his instincts and played a song not even his band mates had heard. The song he played, "Folsom Prison Blues," was completely his own.

The producer had never heard anything like it before. Instead of kicking Johnny out of the studio, he invited him in to produce his first record. Johnny created his own style, and the world loved it. It was completely original and completely his own. He recorded music for the rest of his life and no one could deny his influence. He inspired generations of musicians to make their own mark on the world.

Garth Brooks loved and respected the classic country greats, Johnny Cash, Merle Haggard, and George Jones, but he was also in awe of George Strait. Strait had an ability to write compelling stories. Garth's first breakout hit "Much Too Young

(To Feel This Damn Old)" is a great tune and could have been a George Strait tune. When Garth performs this song, he stands in front of his microphone and delivers the song just like his hero would have done it. With his Stetson hat on, he stays in one spot and sings the song. He mastered the model. But he did not stop there. He evolved into something unique.

There is a reason successful cover bands make considerably less than successful bands with original music. Great cover bands sing the music we know and they belt out the hits one after another, but we pay a great deal more because we want to see the original. We want to hear the stories from the originators. We want to know how they wrote the music and what the music means to them.

We want to see an artist show up and deliver a unique and authentic performance. We do not want to see a copy, because the original is always more valuable. A copy of a famous painting is worth a fraction of the original.

The world needs what you bring to the table and they are willing to pay for it, and wait in line to celebrate it. Authenticity is the spark for invention, innovation, and creativity. It is where some of the craziest ideas come from that change culture.

We were created to do something unique. We were created to be ourselves. We were not created to clone someone else. We already have George Strait; we do not need another one. And if you have ever seen Garth Brooks in concert, he is anything but George Strait. He jumps off the speakers, yells, and performs with everything he has throughout the entire concert. That is his signature creation.

In business, many people stop developing after mastering competence. They find a certain amount of success and feel comfortable. They have found a formula that works. One organization has a successful commercial, and, all of a sudden, their competitors are doing the same. It is what makes many of the ads on television so boring. One of the reasons people enjoy the Super Bowl is because they know they are going to see amazing commercials.

To create your own signature style, reflect on your roots and remember what makes you most proud. I love the line in Garth Brooks's tune "Friends in Low Places" that says, "blame it all on my roots." I believe leaders who reach elevated levels of respect and influence start from their origins. The Beatles sounded much like Buddy Holly, but some of their later experimental albums were nothing like Buddy Holly. Their later albums, *Rubber Soul, Revolver,* and *Sgt. Pepper's Lonely-Hearts Club Band*, are seen as some of the greatest albums of all time. They were creations all their own. Their music did not sound like anyone else. It was the Beatles at their best. During the relatively short window that they performed, they became the largest selling band of all time.

The Bee Gees started out mimicking the Beatles. By the time the disco phenomenon was in full force in the 1970s, the Bee Gees were anything but mimics of the Beatles. The Bee Gees defined disco and created a sound all their own. So, when you are creating your version of success, think about your unique skills and how those skills apply to where you are today. Start to think right now about how you can deliver your core competence in new ways.

Once I decided to focus my career on leadership development, I found a mentor. He had a great family of all daughters just like my family. He also had a great business and was the model for my competence. He was gifted at leadership development and was my coach. I learned to lead and what pitfalls to avoid, and what to pursue. I eventually came up with my own beliefs and strategy. The business I created had a great head start because of his coaching.

When you are developing your own leadership brand, you will find a new energy you never thought possible. You are creating something new, fresh, and unique to you. You are the only one on the planet who can deliver this leadership style. Some of your new ideas will fail miserably, but more often than not, you will see your effectiveness increase because you are being authentic and genuine. This is where the real love of work begins. Prior to this step, you were partly in the shadows, behind the scenes and learning. Now, you are stepping into your leadership potential and seeing new opportunities.

Your uniqueness will attract others who have never seen that side of you, and most will like what they see. Some people will be critics. They were okay when you were following someone else, but now that you are busting out of your shell and showing the world you have something to offer, they will try to find fault.

Eminem was told over and over that what he was doing was garbage. He would have battles with other rappers and get demolished and booed off stage. He did not give up; instead, he kept working on his unique sound. He was inspired by LL Cool J, but he did not stop there. He created a new style of his own. He found his voice and mastered his craft. This process of mastering your unique style takes time, but it is an investment in yourself that always pays off.

In the early days of discovering your signature leadership style, you will have critics, but stick with the plan. When you lead with your unique voice, you are clearing the way for others to do the same. Creating is a harder process than mimicking. When you start creating, you may experience a great deal of fear.

There were hundreds of times I did not want to write this book. I was afraid of what others would say. I would talk to Kristy, my wife, and ask, "How can I write a book about Authentic Confidence when I'm so under confident about it?" That is exactly why I had to write it. The only way we can progress in life is by facing our fears and resolving them. That also makes us the best coaches because we can relate to what others are going through.

In order to love your work, it must become a part of you. After you have mastered the covers, it is time to make an original. Once we master the competence of our mentors, it is time to define our signature style. We must create an authentic version of our craft and then spend the rest of our lives perfecting it. We must know what makes us unique and why that is important to others.

Most people stop at Competence. They find a formula that someone else has created and run with it until the end of their careers. Keep in mind, there is nothing wrong with this approach. If that is the role people want to play, they will simply go back to step one and reduce their expectations around Significance. The cover band will never have the impact of the original, but it is safe, and they still play music.

However, for some people, copying the original is not enough. They realize there is something powerful and magical about creating something authentic. It inspires them to be creative. Pushing through this stage is difficult. It is often met with resistance because few people have reached it; they have not put themselves out there to experience either victory or defeat.

This is a decision point. Will you take the risk? Will you be vulnerable, and will you show the world your true self? It is exactly what those great artists did. Now is the time to find your signature style and lead with authenticity, knowing you are good enough. The original version of you is the best thing you can offer the world. Your life experiences, your genetics, and your preparation have given you a unique voice. Are you willing to share it?

Once you offer your unique competence to the world, you will receive feedback. Remember, you are not as bad as your enemies claim, and you are not as perfect as your mom said you were. The truth lies somewhere in between. As you show the world your authentic version of leadership, those who believe what you believe will rally to you and find ways to help. Those who do not may react in unpredictable ways. Know that this authentic version of you is the healthiest place to live.

When an organization is filled with people looking to contribute their unique gifts to customers, everyone wins. There is something magical that happens when everyone feels that who they are is enough. They do not have to try to be someone else. What they bring is needed and unique and helps the organization win in every way. This is you. It will take some digging and some reflection, but when you find that signature creation that works, you will be ready for the next step, which is leverage. This is where you learn to scale your personal mastery.

A client of mine graduated from a prestigious leadership program. He was excited to go back to his organization and implement what he had learned. Unfortunately, others found the concepts too complicated to implement. He really believed in the power of the principles, but found them hard to apply. After much reflection, he decided to adapt the techniques so they could be implemented in his organization. These adaptations were customized to his situation and the organization loved them. He integrated these principles in key business units with tremendous success. He is now teaching his unique principles in institutions of higher education and is thrilled to be adding on to the work of his heroes.

Once you have learned the skill from your mentor, you will first master it, and then you will make it your own. You cannot help but put your own unique stamp on the skill.

CHAPTER 20

Leverage
(Communicate Confidence)

L earning how to advocate for yourself based on the audience is how you Leverage your leadership. There is a time when leaders need to advocate for themselves. Billy Joel learned this early in his career. He is a musician who's had his struggles in his career. Many people think that Billy Joel wrote his most famous song "Piano Man" after years of struggle, working for tips as a lounge singer. This is not true. He worked at a piano bar for a short time as he was waiting out an unfair recording contract. He had been misled by the recording company and it was a terrible deal. He knew he had to get out of the recording contract, but he still wanted to play music. His strategy was to wait them out. He advocated for himself and decided he would not record any music until they let him out of the contract. So he worked at a place called the Executive Room and that was the inspiration for "Piano Man." Eventually when they realized he was not going to provide any more music, they let him out of the contract, and the rest is history.

The reason why he was able to wait them out was that he knew he was going to have a significant career. He knew he had the talent to make a difference. He was clear about this talent, and he was able to communicate it. Because of his confidence and his ability to demonstrate this confidence clearly, he eventually landed a contract with Columbia records. Columbia was home for artists like Bob Dylan and guided Billy to one of the greatest careers in rock history.

That would not have happened if Billy did not believe in his talents. When record labels are looking for new recording artists, they often talk about the "it" factor. This phrase has always fascinated me. What does "it" mean? I believe part of the "it" factor is when you let the world know you are great at something and you are not afraid to show it.

After you master your new skill in the authenticity stage, it is time to share the news. It is scary because you do not want to appear arrogant, but when communicated effectively, it will elevate your value.

When Billy approached Columbia records, it was clear that he believed in himself and the power of his music. It was his solo contribution that sparked his success, but it has been the power of his band that has kept him relevant in the music scene. He realized that everyone in the band makes up Billy Joel—not just him. His name may be up in lights, but he knows he cannot do it alone.

Several years ago, he decided to test the market by playing a few shows at Madison Square Garden in New York City. Since then, he has sold out twelve shows a year and holds the record for most sold out shows at "The Garden." Everyone in the band has leveraged their skills to make great music, and they are still having a great time playing for their fans. Many of Billy's bandmates have been with him for decades. Many of Billy's contemporaries are not filling stadiums. It is easy to see why. Many veteran musicians change their backing band continually. They will find new players for every tour. It is simply a group of individuals who play together. When this happens, the audience can feel it.

When Billy Joel plays, you can feel the chemistry and the genuine relationships of the band. They have played together for years, and they know their roles and perform at the highest level to ensure the team is a success. Their names may not be in in lights, but it does not mean they are not a critical part of the experience.

Leverage is the intentional process of multiplying your skill. This is where your confidence level and influence will hit new levels of success. People see you as an expert on a subject and doors will open in areas you never thought possible. In the leverage phase, you are no longer apologizing or explaining away your greatness. You are walking into that strength and you own it. People around you take notice because they sense a different level of resolve. It is impressive. You will feel a new sense of influence and resolve. It starts with the inner belief and moves to an external statement of Authentic Confidence.

Many people stop at authenticity, feeling comfortable. They have reached a level of success that is acceptable to them. Remember over 70% of employees are not engaged in their work. Leverage begins when you make the decision to do something meaningful with your work and give your best effort. Leverage goes beyond marginal levels of success and begins to scale beyond your own personal capacity to deliver. You add value to others when you are not in the room. With leverage, your value to the organization escalates and you end up helping customers in ways that previously did not exist.

Because of the authenticity step, you own your style of leadership, which you have worked to perfect. With the addition of leverage, you become laser focused on what you are going to accomplish and what it takes to get there. Action plans become clear, and work becomes satisfying at a level you never knew possible. You cannot wait to get into the office to continue to master your skills and add tremendous value to others.

Every artist I've studied had a great deal of ambition and drive, but they also had a fascination with the work and a desire to serve their fans. They were driven to make sure their fans had an amazing experience with every product or service they delivered. Average was not an option. They wanted every album to be the best album they ever created, and they were always looking forward to the next project. Now, that does not mean that every product or service worked—many did not. It means they believed every project would be a difference maker and would be great for their customers.

I am not advocating an addiction to work or an unhealthy work-life balance. What I am saying is why not make the 75,000 hours that the average person works great? Why not make them productive and significant?

I have met with many high school and college graduates who sought career advice. Many asked me the same question. "How do I make the most amount of money doing the least amount of work?" Then they laughed, and said they were just kidding.

But there's a bit of truth with every "just kidding." We are all looking for easy work.

Once you have mastered an authentic version of your skills, the hard work is done. Now it is time to leverage it. It is time to expand it to serve as many people as possible. Think about music; it is not enough to simply play great live shows. Not everyone will be able to make the trip to watch a musician play. The recording and distribution processes are critical.

You must scale your skills within your organization. This will allow you to reach new levels of confidence. This is intimidating and often will drive under confident behaviors. Taking your skill and applying it to a new area can be challenging.

I regularly teach to the topic of leverage, and I have seen firsthand the transformation that takes place when people come face-to-face with their under confidence issues and, for the first time, conquer their fears. Once you start leveraging your skills in your workplace, your career will begin to thrive. Be patient, however, because it might take some time.

Leverage is the process of becoming equally comfortable with your greatness and weakness. When you communicate your greatness with confidence—not cockiness—you will see your influence expand. Once you resolve a confidence issue, you must learn how to communicate your newfound competence. This is what ignites leverage.

For example, if you resolved an issue around conflict resolution, you might say, "I used to hate conflict, but I'm more comfortable with it now. Let me know if you need any help." You might eventually say, "Conflict used to be a major challenge for me; now, it has become an essential skill."

These phrases communicate your success in this area. They will start to see you as a subject matter expert. If you back it up with a strong delivery of the competence, you will gain influence. You are not pretending that you have always been great in this area but, rather, confidently communicating that you are great now. That is not over confidence; it is clarity.

The fastest road to trust is aligning your confidence and competence and communicating that alignment accurately. Success is built on trust, and you will have made some major deposits in that area.

It is not about telling the world you are a better human being. This approach will decrease your leverage. In other words, you should never say, "I used to be terrible at this, but now I'm a lot better than you are." This pits you against your coworkers and creates a win/lose environment. It starts with an internal belief that you are great and translates into an external statement of service.

When starting on the leverage journey, I often recommend discussing the greatness of the team and the successes you are having. You might say something like, "We have a great team, doing some great work in this area." Eventually, you will find your style of communicating your strengths without sounding like a showoff. It takes practice and some trial and error, but it is so freeing when you finally find your voice at work.

I had been working with one client for years while she was building her skillset. Every time a new book on her area of expertise came out, she was immersed in it. She took on big initiatives at work, some with great success and some with failure. She was resilient, though, in her efforts to keep pushing herself to improve.

After years of doing this, her reputation started to grow. People outside the organization heard of the great work she was doing and people started to solicit for her ideas. Eventually, another organization pursued her and because of her newfound expertise and experience, she was able to earn a substantial increase in her income and the work was amazingly interesting and right in her wheelhouse. She is having more fun than ever and is so thankful she made the decision to pursue her personal and professional growth.

The ideas to leverage your skill will often happen when you are looking for opportunities to add value. As the opportunities arise, your value to the organization will continue to rise and you will find more and more satisfaction from your work. You will see your level of influence increase with your team and your customers. The pride you feel in your work will be contagious to those around you, which will indirectly set the stage for their development.

Leverage is the fun stage of your journey toward living with Authentic Confidence. This is when you learn to accept that you are now skilled in an area that used to be a struggle. It is now time for you to take ownership of this skill. You must not diminish your role in order to take pride in your work in this area. You will learn how to share with others that you are not only competent in this area, but also willing to use this skill to help others. This is where your value in your team and organization will continue to rise. This is where salary increases and promotions become a reality.

For example, one client with whom I worked struggled with project management, and after resolving his confidence issues, he became a great project manager. He was able to solve complicated problems and design a project management strategy that pulled everyone together. Leaders in the organization witnessed this transformation and began handing him new challenging projects that allowed him to showcase his talents.

He was uncomfortable with the newfound encouragement in the beginning, but he learned to accept the praise. He realized that if he wanted his team to take credit for their hard work, then he must model that same behavior. He felt arrogant at first but then learned it was really Authentic Confidence. It was not that he thought he was better than anyone else, but he finally believed it was OK for him to take ownership of the belief that he is a great project manager. He was promoted to a key position in the organization and his influence continues to grow.

CHAPTER 21

Empathy
(Better Together)

mpathy is never forgetting where you came from. It is the belief that even though you may be better at a skill, it does not make you a better person. When Adele won the 2016 Grammy for album of the year, she went on stage and was very emotional as she thanked everyone and accepted the award. I was amazed as I watched her turn to Beyoncé in the crowd and say, "I can't possibly accept this award, and I'm very humbled, and I'm very grateful and gracious, but the artist of my life is Beyoncé," she stated as the crowd cheered. "And this album to me, the *Lemonade* album, was just so monumental, Beyoncé, so monumental, and so well thought out, and so beautiful and soul-baring, and we all got to see another side to you, that you don't always let us see...You are our light, and the way that you make me and my friends feel, the way that you make my black friends feel, is empowering, and you make them stand up for themselves. And I love you, I always have, and I always will." The crowd erupted with cheers for an emotional Beyoncé, verifying Adele's comments. Adele is an amazing artist; yet, in that moment, she recognized greatness in someone else. It was a beautiful example of how genuine humility can propel greatness in others. She was still proud of her album and acknowledged her personal struggles to get there, yet she gave respect to someone she believed deserved the credit.

Unfortunately, not all artists followed this last step. Oasis as a band demonstrated far more judgment than empathy. However, many artists showed tremendous empathy. Sir Paul McCartney has achieved massive success with the Beatles as well as with the band Wings and as a solo artist. With this type of sustained success, it wouldn't surprise anyone if Paul thought he was better than others.

Many consider the Beatles to be the greatest rock and roll band of all time, and he has certainly earned enough money and awards to last a lifetime. But Paul, a boy from Liverpool, never forgot where he came from.

He grew up in hard times and remembers his humble beginnings. He remembers scraping together enough money to see Bill Haley and His Comets perform "Rock Around the Clock." He remembers watching that concert and committing his life to music. He also remembers his own struggles as an early rock and roll band and has compassion for others starting out.

In 2014, he won a Grammy for Best Rock Song with Dave Grohl, Pat Smear, and Krist Novoselic for the song "Cut Me Some Slack." Paul partnered with these younger artists because he considers it a privilege to create music with younger generations. He's still leveraging his skills as an artist and has clearly entered the Empathy phase of his career.

The artists who were able to transition into empathy had the most rewarding end to their careers. Be aware that once you reach a certain level of success, it is tempting to embrace the hype.

Some of the artists were surrounded by poor influences and followed a path that led to isolation and destructive habits. Many of the artists we studied were miserable after reaching the height of their success. However, it does not have to be this way. The artists who continued to find success rewarding had trusted friends and transitioned from leverage into empathy.

This is truly the joy of entering the stage of empathy. It is no longer about what you can create, but what you can help others create. Once you have mastered the first four steps of the Career Confidence Guide: Significance, Confidence, Authenticity and Leverage, you can begin to relax and focus on helping others. Empathy is the mindset that leads to a desire to give back. The goal is for the student to eventually become the teacher and pass on the same confidence-building process to others.

One person I worked with had a tremendous fear of speaking in public and, specifically, standing up in front of others in a training role. She even selected her college major based on never having to take a public speaking course. Ironically, she selected a career where training became a major responsibility.

After she overcame this confidence issue, she not only became competent in her role, but she learned to love it. She dug in and figured it out, and, today, she is a great coach to her co-workers. She is the first to step in and provide strategies and techniques that she learned to deliver great training. The student has now become the teacher, and it is so fun to watch her give back to others in such a meaningful way.

Growing up, I was very close with my grandparents. They were amazing people. The family planned a party for my grandpa when he turned 90. I could tell he was a little nervous.

He was a seasoned farmer from Viroqua, Wisconsin, and life had not been easy. He raised seven children and had a hard life. I could tell he was wondering what this birthday party would be like. It seemed to me as though he knew this might be one of the last times his entire family would be together.

The rest of us were looking at it as though we were honoring a king, but I think he was a little unsure. It was as if he were wondering, "How did I do with this life I was given?"

Well, the day finally arrived, and it was the first time in many years that all of my aunts, uncles, and cousins were together. I couldn't believe the response. Everyone was doing their best to celebrate this man's life. Some sang songs and many shared stories. Grandpa was emotional that day, as everyone shared the impact he had on their lives.

I will never forget one line that was shared; "If you wonder how you did with your life, look around this room. We are all better people because you were in our lives."

One of my colleagues taught me that **the true secret to loving your work is learning to love yourself and sharing that gift with others.** You were placed on this planet for a reason, and only you can do what you do. You have to own it! The world does not need another cover band; it needs originals. It needs you to believe you are more than OK, more than alright. Just look around; people are looking for a leader who will inspire them to greatness. Be the leader you would want to follow. When you transition from finding confidence to coaching confidence, you will help others love their work, and they will love you for it.

For a FREE Career Confidence Guide, visit Confidencekit.BenFauske.com.

If you would like to complete the interactive version of the process covered in this book, visit MyAuthenticConfidence. com and sign up for Authentic Confidence Online. In this video series, I walk through the entire process step by step. I provide a guided experience with an interactive workbook. Enter the code DREAM2020 and receive a discount.

CONCLUSION

Stories of Authentic Confidence

Change of Perception

The team was embarrassed about their reputation. They had lived in the shadows for far too long and they wanted to make a statement. Other departments were working hard to keep the team in their current box. The message was, "You are the doers of the organization, nothing more. You are not strategic or innovative." The team disagreed. They were smart, they were organized, and they added great value. So how would they convince their internal customers?

We started by identifying the confidence issues that were holding the team back. They had years of history to overcome. They had been branded by another leader as transactional, which meant they were not influencers. They did not want to be mean or vindictive, but they needed a shift. Many of the team members were disengaged and did not feel appreciated by the organization.

To make the cultural shift, the team knew they must be aligned. After completing the Authentic Confidence process,

157

they realized the new culture they wanted to create. The way they viewed themselves changed, and, in return, the ways others viewed them changed. They were growing their reputation and adding strategic value.

They had an internal resource that was trained in the Authentic Confidence process and implemented the cultural shift across this entire international department. Engagement has increased and the value proposition has been clearly communicated and delivered.

Team members are now proud of the work and growing reputation of the department and they are continuing to add significant value to their partners and customers.

Own Your Style of Confidence

One organization wanted a strategy to better empower women in the organization. They had many sessions and learning opportunities for this effort. They found the Authentic Confidence process to be one of the most effective sessions.

Many of the women shared the difficulty of learning to lead strong without being perceived as too aggressive. The group was attended by women and men and the discussion led to many practical strategies for team members to find their voice and work. They learned to own their style of confidence.

There are many differences in how confidence is perceived. We discussed how men and women communicate confidence differently. Often, behaviors described as confident for men are described as over confident for women. We started great conversations about the impact of bias and pathways forward. A key strategy to our session was having women and men share honestly about their confidence journeys and seeking input from each other to ensure perception matched reality.

We discussed how confidence and competence work for each individual and how we often sabotage our own success. This was invaluable for leaders at all levels to learn they are not alone when they feel under confident. We found creating a safe environment where women and men can share their confidence experiences often provides clarity for options moving forward.

Leader Won't Change

One of the most common responses I hear when coaching others on confidence is a variation of, "When my leader chooses to lead, I will lead. Until then, I am stuck." I was working with one client on this and she was becoming very frustrated. Whenever a courageous move was needed by the leader, he would fold. Because of this, issues would fester and the culture was regressing.

After going through the Authentic Confidence coaching process, she moved out of the stress of waiting for her leader to change and moved into the clear position of choice. She found her voice and would clearly lay out options for her leader and ask him to choose. Once she learned to challenge and support instead of always challenging, her leader become more open to her ideas and influence. This allowed their relationship to flourish, and he started to make better decisions. Only until she let go of the need to judge did she really communicate confidence.

She now is supporting a massive culture shift with the full support of her leader and the rest of the organization. She has launched several strategies that are dramatically enhancing the culture and increasing employee engagement. Her efforts are continually enhancing the lives of every employee and she found an influence she never thought possible with her current leader.

Out of the Comfort Zone

One leader I worked with was struggling with chronic confidence issues. No matter what feedback others gave her, she was not convinced that addressing conflict and taking a risk was worth it. She had a good job and was respected by others and life was going well.

Only when she was passed over for a significant promotion that she felt she deserved did things change. She was now tired of dragging around her confidence issues. It was time to learn how to let go of the baggage.

We worked through the core confidence issues, and she started to feel the weight lifting. After completing the process, she was leading highly effective team meetings without worry. She was coaching others in the organization who would have intimidated her in the past. She also felt "in-charge" of her career for the first time in her life. She clearly articulated what she wanted out of her career and shared the future vision with her boss.

She is now teaching others how to work through their confidence issues, and the vulnerability of her story is powerful. Her engagement has dramatically increased, and so has the engagement of those she serves.

Relationships Matter

One client I worked with was a genius. When it came to technical issues, he was almost always right. He knew where he wanted to go and how to get there. The problem was many people were not joining him on the ride. Many individuals went to his leader and told her that they wanted to be moved to a different team. He was brilliant, but others did not believe he cared about them. They were simply pawns in his chess game to get the result he wanted.

His leader shared the feedback with him, and he was shocked. He couldn't understand how they did not see his perspective. It was about the work. He would say, "If you get the work done and you perform it with high standards, everyone wins; it is not that complicated. Achieve the results and the organization will serve customers well and we will all be financially rewarded for the success."

Unfortunately, this simple explanation did not resonate with many of his coworkers. As a result, he had to learn how he was being perceived. He went through the Authentic Confidence process and learned that he had a bias toward over confidence, which was affecting his relationships negatively. He identified the phrases he used that people interpreted negatively and had to learn a new language. He wanted to create a culture of accountability instead of resentment and fear.

Fortunately for him, he had a great leader who encouraged his progress along the way. This allowed him the space to improve communication, and, eventually, form much stronger relationships with everyone he worked with.

He is now leveraging his brilliant ideas with others who are receptive and supportive. The engagement scores of those who work with him have dramatically improved. They appreciate his efforts to accept feedback and become a stronger teammate.

Authentic Confidence

No one is born with a bias toward Authentic Confidence. No matter where you are in your journey, you are simply moving more toward Authentic Confidence every day.

One of the leaders I work with was looking for a leadership development platform that matched what he believed and would help move the organization forward. We implemented the Authentic Confidence process in the organization, and, now, he has the language to describe the way he has been leading for years. The organization has embraced the process and has seen drama and gossip decrease and meaningful progress toward a life-changing mission increase.

He has been looking for a coaching framework for years that would address the balance between results and relationships. The organization is learning how to lead with accountability and appreciation. It has become a safe place for individuals to advocate for themselves while keeping the mission of the team as the top priority. The service to their customers continually wins awards, and they are designing life-changing strategic plans for the future.

Hope for Now, Hope for the Future

One comment I hear often is, "As soon as I find a new job, I will love my work." Well, I had eight jobs in eight years and simply moving from one job to another is not the answer. I brought my confidence issues to every new job.

You may need to find a new job, but I always recommend that you resolve your confidence issues first and give it your best in your current position. Then, if after a while, things are still not working, find a new opportunity.

I spent much of my career running away from what I did not want instead of defining what I wanted and going after it. I first learned how to love my work where I was, and then I found opportunities to make that happen. Start now, and you can always move later.

I have found that many individuals who were convinced they needed to leave decided to stay after working through their confidence issues. They realized that much of what they wanted was right where they were; they just needed to do a better job communicating their needs.

Some people say, "Easy for you to say… you work for yourself." This is true, and before I launched Authentic Confidence, I worked for an organization I loved. The company remains one of my clients to this day. The only reason I left is because I did not want to move my family.

You can learn to love your work right where you are. If you give it a fair shot and then decide to move on, you will not regret your decision. I just do not want you to walk away from something that may end up being a great fit for you. Even when you are dealing with the parts of your job that are not fun, you will be doing it with people whom you have learned to appreciate. You will create a culture where you all have permission and safety to be your authentic selves.

Imagine the relationships working, your influence increasing… Imagine receiving fair compensation, being selected for that challenging new project, or receiving the promotion you always wanted. How would your personal life change if you were valued for your contributions? What would it look like for you to walk into work every day loving what you do and feeling safe? What would it feel like to address your confidence issues and support others on the team overcoming their own challenges? What would it feel like to communicate clearly where you add value to your team and the organization? What if your customers became your friends? What if it could happen in your current organization? Career wealth is how you define it. What if you start doing what you want to do and being valued fairly for that contribution?

If you have tried everything and it is still not working, you can always transition. Then when you do, you will know you are moving toward something you want, instead of away from something you hate. You will know you did everything you could to make it work. You have done your internal work and it is time to move on. Then you will be excited about the next opportunity. Just as in relationships, if we do not work on our issues, we will simply take them with us to the next relationship.

No matter where you are in your confidence journey, enhancing your relationships is the greatest impact you can have on the culture of your organization. When you are driving out of the parking lot of your organization for the last time, what will be your legacy? Coaching confidence in others has been the greatest privilege in my career, and I hope you will join me in building a world where leaders live and lead with Authentic Confidence. Our teammates, families, and customers are worth it. All the best.

ACKNOWLEDGMENTS

Simon Sinek, David Mead, Bob Chapman, Brian Wellinghoff, Donald Miller, Jeff Walker, Michael Hyatt, Dr. Gary Chapman, Dr. Craig Malkin and Brené Brown, you have been my mentors from a distance. Thanks for being committed to the work of helping people live fulfilled and wholehearted lives.

Dean Peterson, you set the framework for great coaching. I will never forget your words of encouragement.

Jon Syndergaard, you have been a rock. Your belief in me and launching the beginnings of Authentic Confidence is a decision I will never forget.

Rob Hathaway, you have been an amazing friend and advisor. Your wisdom and insights have been invaluable, and I can't thank you enough.

Beth Aldana and Mel Lewis, thanks for pushing me and challenging me to the next level. You both taught me the power of cocreation and I can't wait for the future.

Thanks to Steve Kuper for supporting my start in this coaching journey. Your generosity to me and others is exceptional. Thank you.

JJ Eaton, you have been a tremendous guide for me. Your wisdom and insight forged my path in business and life. Thanks for showing me what it means to be a leader. Boom.

Thanks Don Murphy, for helping me out and believing in the vision. You keep me headed in the right direction. You are the best.

I am grateful for Jeremy Goodfellow, who believed in my work and challenged me to do something about it. This nudge started the book-writing process and has meant more to me than you will ever know (I guess now you know).

Denis Caron, your belief in me and my future inspired me to keep moving forward. Thanks for keeping me curious.

Thanks to Diane Sawyer who provided brilliant insight into the importance of confidence issues at work. Thank you for shedding more light on an incredibly important topic and encouraging me to go for it.

Wendy Naarup, your encouragement and countless hours of dedication to this project inspired me every day. This project is a result of your efforts to pay it forward in life.

I can't thank Rick and Laurie Schinke enough for being the best business advisors and friends. You have set an amazing example of what it means to help.

Brian Berggren is a great designer and an even better friend. You have the gift of translating ideas into design. I am proud to have your design work in this book.

I appreciate Michael and David Cuene, and you too, Paula Kuse. Your commitment to culture and leadership is inspiring and I am looking forward to the places we will go.

The St. Norbert College and the Center for Exceptional Leadership team: Dan Heiser, Dean Stewart, Angela Marshalek (you are special), Suzanne Lyons and Karen Del Marcelle. You are a great team, thanks for your investment in me as a leader and, more important, as a person. Special thanks to Dave Wegge and Grant Rozeboom, fellow journeyers in the cause.

Patrick and Jess Dewane, Aric and Liz Thoreson, Kevin and Denise Wood, you have all been amazingly supportive and an important part of this project.

My clients are also my friends. Many thanks to Broadway Automotive, Encapsys, Government Finance Officers Association, CP, the City of Appleton, the City of Green Bay, the City of Oshkosh, JJ Keller, KASD, Schreiber Foods, US Venture, Sanimax, UWGB, Winnebago and others.

Mary Goggins, Myriah Farrell, Chris Morrill, Tim Hanna, Eric Genrich, Joe Faulds, Mark Rohloff, John Fitzpatrick, Mary McNevin, Cristi Burrell, Jenene Calloway, John Matz, Lara Vendola, Eric Trudeau, Diane Trudel, Donn Johnson, Kelly Montonati, Ryan Kauth, Diane Welhouse, Julie Kozicke, Brad Grant, Mark Duerwaechter and Chris McDaniel.

I had some great guidance from Morgan James Publishing, Peaceful Media, Lise Cartwright, Lizette Balsdon, Christos Angelidakis, Gabe Dahl, Kari Hanula Jr., Jen Stevenson, Laureen Endter, Ellen Kunz, Wayne Purdin, Adam Demetrician, Gary Smith and STV Advisors. Stan and Janet Koplien, Aaron and Sarah Fauske, Kelly and Tim Williams, Angela and James Jones, Dustin and Katie Koplien, and all the kids. Your belief in the work created an amazing environment for this project. Last but not least, thanks to all the leaders I have had the privilege of working with whom I consider my heroes: you know who you are, and you demonstrate Authentic Confidence every day.

RESOURCES

Authentic Confidence Online

If you are interested in personally implementing this process, Authentic Confidence Online will provide step by step instructions. This video series is taught by Creator and Coach Ben Fauske. You will learn your Confidence Profile; complete your Authentic Confidence Quotient, and Career Confidence Guide. There are also bonus materials and Weekly Confidence Boosters. Thousands have experienced significant growth in their careers after completing this course. Sign up for Authentic Confidence Online at MyAuthenticConfidence.com. Enter the Code: DREAM2020 to receive your discount.

Authentic Confidence Coach

Learn how to find confidence in all areas of your career and coach confidence in others. Coaching Authentic Confidence is the highest form of influence. Learn the process and share the information with those you serve. Visit BenFauske.com/services to schedule your FREE consultation.

Authentic Confidence Live

If you would like to engage your team in the process, schedule your Authentic Confidence Live workshop. This interactive day will ensure everyone on your team understands how to find, communicate, and coach with Authentic Confidence. Visit BenFauske.com/services for more information.

ABOUT THE AUTHOR

Ben Fauske is invested in serving leaders so that great teams thrive. He is a confidence researcher who equips individuals with the tools to build their ideal careers. His clients describe him as passionate and committed to their success. Thousands of leaders have used the Authentic Confidence Process to build the careers and teams they deserve. The process creates a coaching culture in organizations that drives employee engagement and customer confidence. Ben is also the Consulting Leader for the Center for Exceptional Leadership at St. Norbert College.

Prior to founding RISE Leadership and creating the Authentic Confidence Process, Ben was the Director of Organizational Development for a Canadian based multinational corporation. He led talent development and leadership training from the executive level to the shop floor.

Ben is a Certified Professional Behavioral Analyst and Trainer. He is sought after for executive coaching, workshops, and keynotes. For additional information, visit BenFauske.com.